Sustainable Champions

How International Companies are Changing
the Face of Business in China

FU JIA
JONATHAN GOSLING
& MORGEN WITZEL

SUSTAINABLE
CHAMPIONS

**HOW INTERNATIONAL
COMPANIES
ARE CHANGING
THE FACE OF
BUSINESS IN CHINA**

Routledge
Taylor & Francis Group

LONDON AND NEW YORK

First published 2015 by Greenleaf Publishing Limited

Published 2017 by Routledge
2 Park Square, Milton Park, Abingdon, Oxon OX14 4RN
711 Third Avenue, New York, NY 10017, USA

Routledge is an imprint of the Taylor & Francis Group, an informa business

Cover by Arianna Osti (ariannaosti.com)

British Library Cataloguing in Publication Data:
    A catalogue record for this book is available from the British Library.

        ISBN-13: 978-1-78353-160-8 [pbk]
        ISBN-13: 978-1-78353-161-5 [hbk]

Contents

Figures

Tables

Boxes

Foreword
Sustainability champions in China

China's modern development has delivered more people out of poverty in an equivalent time than in any period or place in human history. Foreign direct investment into China has been an essential aspect of its recent development, and the associated businesses have therefore contributed to China's economic and broader social success. China's declared policy since the early 1980s of "Going Out" has opened it to international capital, technology and businesses in driving an export and infrastructure-led development pathway.

Multinationals over the same period have evolved to embrace a wider set of responsible business practices across their global operations, from their management of labour standards in global supply chains to new standards on everything from anti-bribery to pollution and carbon emissions, and to the disclosure on their sustainable development policies, capabilities and impacts. Such practices have often in their initial stages been adopted in the face of public pressure, indeed often because of perceptions of poor sustainability performance in China and elsewhere.

Over time, responsible business practices have become embedded in international corporate leading norms, although they remain far from being universally adopted despite many new standards being developed and advocated. Where successfully adopted, they have become a keystone in securing not only high public regard, but also the best employees, good government relations, and innovative and productive cultures that in turn drive business success. Multinationals have led in bringing such practices to China, partly because they have become company-wide standards, but also increasingly because of growing demands from the Chinese public and the state.

China was initially reluctant to accept, let alone emulate, international responsible business standards that went beyond Chinese law and norms. Since the turn of the century, China's larger businesses, especially those with growing outward investments and international brand profiles, began to adopt such standards. Most recently, and partly in response to serious concerns among the Chinese public about domestic environmental and social challenges, growing numbers of Chinese companies have moved beyond emulation and started driving sustainable development into the DNA of their businesses. This latter development, strengthened in China's forward-looking policy context of the "new normal", which emphasizes development quality over quantity, is providing a new source of innovative leadership practices which should in turn shape the next generation of international, sustainability-aligned business practices.

The evolution of responsible business practices in China is a keystone of our recent economic, and broader, international history, and it is timely that the role of multinationals in this context is explored and better understood. The leadership experiences set out in such practical and compelling fashion in this book illuminate this role, highlighting how practice has been shaped by a combination of international and domestic drivers, together with personal leadership and determined managerial actions. The book's blend of practical storytelling and evidence-based analysis should inspire and provide a rich source of lessons for students and managers and also policy-makers seeking to enhance the role of business in society, in China and internationally.

Dr Simon Zadek
Distinguished Fellow, Academy of Business in Society
Visiting Scholar, Tsinghua School of Economics and Management
Non-resident Senior Fellow, Chongyang Institute for
Financial Studies, Renmin University of China
Co-Director, UNEP Inquiry into the Design
of a Sustainable Financial System

Acknowledgements

The research underpinning this book derives from detailed interviews with key informants in the companies and WWF China, gathered over five years of continuous engagement funded by a number of independent sources – including the University of Exeter, WWF Norway and WWF China. The three co-authors – experts in supply chain, leadership and organizational change – have been intimately involved from the start and so have others who contributed significant insight to background research and modelling the innovation processes: especially Professor John Bessant and Dr Anna Trifilova, both with wide experience of corporate innovation around the world; and Professor Zhaohui Wu of Oregon State University. In addition to this multidisciplinary research team, the Executive Programme Director and Climate Savers Programme Manager at WWF China, Dr Lin Li and Xin Chen, day-to-day campaigners and negotiators in the field, have steered, criticized and encouraged this work with a focused intent. Additionally we thank Mr Yu Gong, one of our PhD students, who provided writing support on the Yingli and Vanke case studies. We are also tremendously grateful to the 60 executives and managers in the companies described here for their time and generosity in meeting with us, sometimes repeatedly, arranging access to their plants and offices, and granting us licence to write freely as we found things.

Introduction

Can growth and sustainability be combined? The best place to look for an empirical answer is China because the scale is so large on both counts. Economic growth has slowed but remains impressive (GDP grew by US$1.5 trillion between 2012 and 2014);[1] but equally important is the nature of this activity: consumers are becoming more brand-conscious, alert to values as well as value. It is no longer enough to produce cheaply and consistently: brand positioning is crucial even in the third- and fourth-tier cities served by satellite TV and global-level advertising. Along with discerning consumers, multinational companies face stiff competition from a state sector that enjoys a low cost of capital, and a dynamic, agile and well-networked private sector, including several Chinese multinationals. Even national players can be significant competitors – China's three largest provinces (Guangdong, Jiangsu and Shandong) would each figure in the world's top 20 national economies.[2] All of these consumers, and all these companies, are clamouring for growth.

1   As calculated by the National China Statistical Bureau.
2   According to the International Monetary Fund (IMF).

At the same time, the impetus for sustainable modes of business is coming from all directions. Once championed by a few meddlesome non-governmental organizations (NGOs) and cautious scientists, now citizens, employees, customers, governments and business leaders know sustainable growth is the way forward, underpinning the social legitimacy of growth. Waking up day after day to the smoggy haze enveloping Beijing and many other cities, sustainability has an aesthetic, visceral meaning: we have cut ourselves off from clean air, the blue sky and sunshine.

China's environmental crisis is one of the most pressing challenges to emerge from the country's rapid industrialization. Its economic rise, which has averaged around 10% annual GDP growth for the past decade, has come at the expense of its environmental and public health. As the world's largest source of carbon emissions, China is responsible for a third of the planet's greenhouse gas (GHG) output and has 16 of the world's 20 most polluted cities. Life expectancy in the north has decreased by 5.5 years due to air pollution, and severe water contamination and scarcity have compounded land deterioration problems. Environmental degradation cost the country roughly 9% of its gross national income in 2008, according to the World Bank,[3] threatening to undermine the country's growth and exhausting public patience with the government's pace of reform. It has also bruised China's international standing as the country expands its global influence, and endangered its stability as the ruling party faces increasing media scrutiny and public discontent.[4] Sustainability is the urgent need and basic

---

3   Retrieved from http://www.worldbank.org/content/dam/Worldbank/ document/SR3--229-292.pdf.

4   Xu, B. (2014). China's environmental crisis. Retrieved from http://www.cfr. org/china/chinas-environmental-crisis/p12608.

standard for all innovation. It is acutely important for any company, global or domestic, to do business in a sustainable way.

There is a big debate over whether corporate-led globalization is a positive or negative force for the environment. Many foreign multinational corporations (MNCs) in China have been targeted by civil society groups for dumping and emitting waste into the air and water, using toxic materials in the manufacturing process and abusing labour rights. This book shines a light on the conversation about whether foreign direct investment in China promotes a sort of "race to the bottom" or if it can elevate environmental and labour standards. Here we have nine case studies featuring companies that are trying to do better, in various ways.

We present case studies of nine large companies operating in China, focusing on sustainability-oriented innovations in their supply chains (Table I.1). Eight of these companies are World Wide Fund for Nature (WWF) Climate Savers, members of a club of multinationals pledged to reduce their greenhouse gas emissions by significant proportions year on year.[5] One, Nestlé, is a member of the Bioplastics Feedstock Alliance (BFA), also coordinated by WWF. These companies work with the global NGO to inform, monitor and accredit their progress. The targets they pursue are global, and it is relatively easy to make improvements in China because the base level is low and the scale enormous. Innovations in China

---

5   WWF Climate Savers is a global leadership platform which positions multinational corporations at the forefront of the low-carbon economy. The member companies set sector-leading targets for greenhouse gas (GHG) reduction in their own emissions and work with other companies, suppliers and partners to implement innovative solutions for a clean, low-carbon economy. Initiated by WWF in 1999, the Climate Savers programme now counts 30 member companies, including Johnson & Johnson, IBM, Nike, Hewlett-Packard, The Collins Companies, Xanterra Parks and Resorts, Sagawa, Sony, Tetra Pak, Lafarge, Catalyst, Novo Nordisk and Nokia Siemens Networks. All of these companies have pledged to reduce their GHG emissions considerably.

Company	Fairmont Hotels	Hewlett-Packard	Nestlé	SKF	Sony	Tetra Pak	Vanke	Volvo Group	Yingli
Sector	Hospitality/hotel	IT	Food processor	Engineering	Consumer electronics	Packaging	Real estate	Automotive	Clean technology (photo-voltaic)
Country of origin	Canada	USA	Switzerland	Sweden	Japan	Sweden	China	Sweden	China
First established in China	2009	1982	1990	1988	1996	1979	1984	1992	1987
Nature of Chinese operation	Wholly owned foreign enterprise (WOFE)	WOFE	WOFE and Joint Venture (JV)	WOFE	WOFE	WOFE	HQ in China	WOFE	HQ in China, NYSE listed
Size of Chinese operation	4 hotels; Beijing, Shanghai (Peace) and Kunshan (Yangcheng Lake), Nanjing	China HQ: Beijing; Branch companies in 8 provinces; 1 HP lab; 2 plants in Shanghai and Chongqing; 1 call centre in Dalian	China HQ: Beijing; 21 plants in 10 provinces; 1 lab in Shanghai	China HQ: Shanghai; 11 plants and service companies in China; Global Technical Centre China	China HQ: Beijing; 8 plants; 1 software development centre in Dalian	China HQ: Shanghai; 2 plants (Beijing and Hohhot); Design centre in Foshan	HQ: Shenzhen; branch companies in over 20 provinces; Architecture Research Centre in Dongguan	China HQ: Beijing; branch companies in 22 provinces; 1 R&D centre in Jinan;	HQ: Baoding; 4 plants (Baoding; Hengshui; Hainan; Tianjin)

TABLE I.1   The nine companies featured in the case studies

can translate into significant step-changes in global outcomes. Of course, carbon is only one part of sustainability, and we see in these studies an emphasis on CO_2 and energy efficiency, which is always a good idea for the business bottom line. In addition, we also try to include sustainable practices that go beyond CO_2 emissions.

The innovations described here should be understood in this wider context. Global strategies translate into national programmes, and these are mediated by many factors external to corporate management: national and regional governments, industry regulation, consumer pressure groups and environmental NGOs among them. But country managers do more than simply adopt global strategies: they influence and sometimes create new strategies through the practical actions they take, responding to local conditions. In smaller emerging economies, these local adaptations usually stay local; but in China the scale and dynamism are enough to drive change with global significance. The innovations emerging from the front line of production, sourcing, assembly, marketing, consumption and disposal make substantial differences to the overall environmental performance of these firms; they often influence practices up and down the supply chain; and they set new standards for corporate practice. These operational aspects of business management are opportunities for managers to get things right – to solve problems, make new connections and even to invent new business models. So in this book we concentrate on what managers can do. Our aim is to inspire and inform action. But it is not all positive – there are failures and shortcomings along the way, and we have drawn out some lessons from these too.

In the concluding chapter we present a brief literature review of sustainable supply chain management (SSCM) as it relates to the case studies in this book, in order to link together the innovative examples presented with the wider ongoing discussion surrounding SSCM best practice. This chapter will give practising managers and students valuable insight into the wider research context.

The corporate contexts

These are all companies with centrally defined sustainability strategies, which is why they joined the WWF Climate Savers and signed up to public targets for improved efficiencies, reduced carbon footprint and energy savings. These translate in the Chinese context to "framework" strategies which set the direction for innovation – for example, Tetra Pak's "4Rs" (renewing, reducing, recycling, responsibility), Sony's "Road to Zero" and Vanke's "Three Star System" offer shaping slogans and messages within which specific actions can be deployed.

However, these must be more than aspirational slogans: companies place considerable emphasis on measurement and benchmarking across their global operations, and Chinese plants are included in this competitive process. These case studies provide detailed accounts of specific innovations, including the processes by which changes have been implemented. A useful way to categorize these is by reference to the "innovation space" that they address (see Table I.2).

Innovation target	Examples
Product/service offering	"Green" products, design for greener manufacture and recycling, service models replacing consumption/ownership models
Process innovation	Improved and novel manufacturing processes, lean systems inside the organization and across supply chain, green logistics
Position innovation	Rebranding the organization as "green", meeting needs of underserved communities – e.g. bottom of pyramid
"Paradigm" innovation – changing business models	System-level change, multi-organization innovation, servitization (moving from manufacturing to service emphasis)

TABLE I.2 Sustainability-led innovation mapped onto innovation space framework

Source: Trifilova, A., Bessant, J., Jia, F., & Gosling, J. (2013). Sustainable innovation and the Climate Savers programme: experiences of international companies in China. *Corporate Governance*, 13(5), 599-612.

This categorization distinguishes the kinds of change aimed at improving products, processes, positioning or the overall business model. Readers of this book will find it helpful to look out for the intended and actual impacts in each case. In the Volvo Group case, for example, new packaging for component handling processes was beneficial to the Volvo Group and drove similar improvements up their supply chain. In others, the innovation quickly extended beyond original intentions – for example, Vanke's plan for a "green building" led them to develop standards for the entire industry sector. Nonetheless, managers will do well to clarify their intended innovation space, and to plan accordingly. This will help with practical matters of budgeting and project planning; it will also help them notice when they are being drawn out of that space. For example, you want to make sure you get your own process improvement bedded in, but competition might force you to reposition your offering for new markets – as happened to the Fairmont Hotel featured in this book. Alternatively, you might hope to attract new consumers, but find your attention taken up with improving the sustainability of basic material production – as happened to Nestlé in one stage of the developments described here. So this framework can help you focus where you want to innovate, and also alert you to changes in potential impact.

Managerial activism is a significant feature of these case studies. The commitment to more sustainable practices has already been made at the highest levels, and the people we meet in these case studies are driving the agenda in their companies and sometimes beyond. But it is worth asking whether these changes are really going to save the planet: does it matter that Volvo recycles its packaging if its trucks are still belching carbon into the atmosphere? Our view is unequivocally positive: yes, it is good to do what we can, and each step changes the situation, opening unexpected opportunities. The important message of this book is that managers can and should improve the environmental and social performance of their companies. Bigger transformations are on the way, and this is one way of making them go well.

However, there are clearly differences in the level of ambition that motivates sustainable innovation. While some are excited by the possibilities of entirely new waves of innovation forced into being by the social, economic and environmental pressures facing the planet, others prefer to focus on finding better ways to do what they are already doing. Table 1.3 sets out a simple framework describing three levels of ambition; none of the companies in this book is

Level	Characteristics	Examples
0 Passive/ cosmetic	No activity, or "cosmetic" public relations-based statements of intent	n/a
1 Improvement innovation	"Do what we do but better" innovation, taking waste out, reducing footprint of existing processes, efficiency enhancing	Compliance with externally imposed regulation Commitment to frameworks such as FSC Greening of existing processes, products and inter-organizational value chains
2 Opportunity-driven innovation	Creation of new products, processes, services which open up innovation space	New technologies – solar, etc. New process routes and architectures – e.g. low-energy bioprocessing instead of thermal cracking
3 System-level innovation	Creation of new business models at system level involving reframing of the way value is created and often extending across multiple organizations	Interface Flor reinventing itself as an integrated "green" company

TABLE 1.3   Levels of sustainability-oriented innovation

Source: Trifilova, A., Bessant, J., Jia, F., & Gosling, J. (2013). Sustainable innovation and the Climate Savers programme: experiences of international companies in China. *Corporate Governance*, 13(5), 599-612.

at Level 0, doing nothing. Several are actively engaged at Level 1, reducing the footprint of their current operations and cleaning their supply chain. Some pitch straight in at Level 2, opening up an innovation space in new products, processes or markets (as described in Table I.2 above). Several start out at Level 1 and then find themselves setting up new businesses, as Tetra Pak found with its recycling initiatives in cities around China. Few set out at Level 3, but in this collection we present at least one candidate – Yingli, a manufacturer of photovoltaic cells. Seizing the opportunity of a new technology and massive demand for clean energy, and backed by the government, this large start-up aimed to disrupt energy markets and dominate this new global sector.

These two frameworks are helpful analytical tools, but, as the case studies show, no company fits neatly into one level or one innovation space. Most don't even fit into just one sector; for example, when Tetra Pak opened a vast new aseptic packaging plant in Hohhot, Inner Mongolia, it was obliged by the regional government to source all its energy from renewables. There was nowhere near enough capacity at the time, so Tetra Pak found itself investing in energy generation, and thus impacting the local energy markets. Similarly (though on a much smaller scale), Fairmont Hotels set out to serve locally grown organic vegetables, and when the farm became a tourist destination in its own right, they developed a new service delivering fresh organic produce to homes in nearby Shanghai. One thing that becomes clear in these case studies is that innovation occurs not just in a company or even a supply chain; it is part of an industrial ecology in which sustainability is becoming a ubiquitous theme.

The role of WWF

WWF China was established in 1980, the first international NGO invited by central government to operate in China. Funded largely by WWF organizations in northern Europe, the UK and the United States, it has focused on fulfilling global programmes on biodiversity, climate change, ecosystem protection and so forth. WWF Climate Savers is a global programme that seeks to transform businesses into leaders of the low-carbon economy. The intention of the programme is to inspire a change in thinking about climate solutions in leading companies and as agents of change within their sphere of influence. This leaves member companies better placed to avoid carbon-related risks while realizing opportunities in their long-term business strategies. They do this in a number of "front-stage" and "back-stage" activities. Front-stage activities include knowledge exchanges, staff training and profile and reputation enhancement. Back-stage, WWF experts are engaged in regulatory policy, environmental standards and climate negotiations. They are probably one of the more corporate-friendly environmental NGOs, with a long tradition of seeking to engage, persuade and facilitate change. But they are also a formidable campaigning voice, and their Panda logo – among the world's best-known brands – attests to their long and prominent engagement in China.

One fruit of this partnership is that Climate Savers Programme Managers in WWF China have strong relationships with counterparts in the Climate Saver companies, and these partners were receptive to the offer to learn from a formal and independent review of their experiences. Hence this book came into being.

Using the case studies

The authors have used these case studies in MBA and Master's courses on three continents, and several are published through the Case Centre (www.thecasecentre.org). The versions published here are adapted to provide ready examples for practising managers in China and elsewhere, without the need for teaching notes. A summary of the case study is provided at the end of each chapter.

1
Responsible tourism: Fairmont Hotels

1.1 Introduction

Fairmont Hotels & Resorts was founded in 1907. Its first hotel, the landmark Fairmont San Francisco, became the city's venue of choice for glittering balls and presidential visits. Today the Fairmont portfolio includes the Fairmont Banff Springs, the Savoy in London, Quebec City's Château Frontenac and New York's The Plaza. Fairmont has grown into a leading luxury global hotel company with over 56 destinations.

Fairmont was also the first hotel chain to operate in a socially and environmentally sustainable fashion, long before "corporate social responsibility" became a buzzword. Fairmont Canadian hotels pioneered the Green Partnership programme in 1990, and this was then rolled out across the company. Today, Fairmont's sustainability programme encompasses activities such as recycling, organic waste diversion in the hotels' kitchens, retrofitting energy-efficient lighting, redistribution of household goods and food to those in need, purchasing green power and employing sustainable energy technology.

Fairmont's green philosophy is now one of the core values of the company. It is the first global hotel brand to join forces with the World Wide Fund for Nature (WWF) and become part of its Climate Savers programme. This programme establishes ambitious voluntary targets to address climate change. Climate Saver companies will collectively cut carbon emissions by 14 million tonnes annually – the equivalent of taking more than 3 million cars off the road every year – and at the same time these companies will save hundreds of millions of dollars in energy costs.

In 2009, Fairmont announced that it had pledged to reduce operational CO_2 emissions from its existing portfolio of hotels by 20% below 2006 levels by 2013. New Fairmont properties would aim to reduce their CO_2 emissions through the implementation of the company's new Energy and Carbon Management programme. Reducing emissions by 20% equates to removing 19,777 cars from the road annually, preventing the burning of 174,775 barrels of oil, or avoiding the consumption of 1,004 tanker trucks of gasoline. In addition, WWF and Fairmont agreed that the hotels would:

- Adopt a green procurement policy and supplier code of conduct

- Educate and encourage its top suppliers (representing approximately 25% of the supply chain) to provide products in accordance with the green procurement policy and supplier code of conduct

- Update existing design and construction standards to incorporate and reflect LEED standards[1]

1   Leadership in Energy and Environmental Design (LEED) is a green building certification: see http://www.leed.net.

- Endeavour to include sustainable and LEED-certified hotels across the brand

- Seek to relocate Fairmont Hotels & Resorts corporate offices in Toronto, Canada to a building with a LEED NC Gold target

Under the leadership of Fairmont's corporate environmental affairs division and hotel-based Green Teams, 26,000 Fairmont employees have become environmental ambassadors, helping to protect the habitat, resources and culture of the areas where they and their guests work, live and play. The main focus of the Fairmont Green Partnership programme is on responsible sustainable practices, both at a corporate level and at individual properties. To ensure sustainable operations, Fairmont has embraced policies that minimize impact on the environment by making ongoing operational improvements, mainly in waste management, energy and water conservation.

1.2 Fairmont Hotels in China

Fairmont manages three properties in China under its own brand. The Fairmont Beijing is a newly built hotel where employees believe that "the owner is very energy-conscious and wants to build green hotels in green environments, putting lots of effort in here to make sure that everything is green", according to Hans Hordijk, the former General Manager of the Beijing Fairmont. By contrast, the Fairmont Peace in Shanghai is a renovation of the famous old Shanghai Peace hotel. Because of the age of the building, there have been some limitations and restrictions on efforts to conserve energy. The third is the Fairmont Yangcheng Lake Hotel in Kunshan, in the countryside near Shanghai (we shall describe this hotel in more detail below). Fairmont manages a further eight properties in the country under the Swiss Hotel brand.

Fairmont is trying to bring a new and different culture into the hotel industry by offering guests a unique product, an experience of an environmentally sensitive area and a beautiful location, managed in the most responsible way. Part of Fairmont's company philosophy is the education of both staff and guests about the environment, history and culture of the areas in which it operates. This Fairmont global philosophy has been transferred to China and is being adjusted locally. There are major projects across all the company's properties aimed at conserving energy and reducing energy usage, reducing consumption of gas and water, reducing packaging, recycling kitchen waste and where possible using organic or sustainably sourced food in its restaurants. "Green committees" in every hotel give employees a chance to come up with and implement their own ideas, and also serve as a channel for staff education on sustainability.

1.3 Fairmont environmental initiatives

As well as energy savings, Fairmont's environmental committees developed initiatives on how to make all sorts of reduction in the hotels' consumption of power, gas and water, and in reducing packaging, increasing the use of double-sided printing or refilling used printer cartridges. Recycling is also a major issue. Fairmont China introduced coloured bins in kitchens for vegetable scraps and coffee grinds. All coffee grinds are saved and reused as compost to enrich the soil. "Coffee grinds are really good for the soil," says Philip Smith, general manager of the Yangcheng Lake Hotel. "They help increase acidity. Granules add into the aeration. Since the coffee grinds are rough they allow some air to the soil, and the soil becomes healthy."

Fairmont green committees also promote sustainability in different hotel departments. Each department must be represented on the committee. Representatives discuss environmental initiatives that their departments are working on. Hans Hordijk, former general manager of the Beijing Fairmont, says: "to be successful [the programme] has to be employee-driven rather than management-driven. I can sit here and say you must do this with this item, but if the staffs don't own it, it's not going to happen all the time."

Every green committee comes up with different ideas about sustainability. Often these ideas are then submitted to Fairmont's green e-platform, which allows hotels to share and exchange green ideas. If the idea is implemented it becomes a green initiative. The hotel that submits the most initiatives in a year gets an environmental award.

Philip Smith provides an example:

> In Canada there was an initiative about grey water, which comes from refrigeration. Fridges are cooled by water, and after being used the water goes down the drain. In Canada by law, grey water cannot be used for drinking once it has gone through a machine. The initiative was about rechannelling this cleaned grey water for use in urinals and toilets.

Emily Liu, Assistant Director of Rooms, offers other examples:

> If we find a good idea, we'll disseminate it to other departments wherever possible. For example, we have a battery recycling station in each department and will hand the collected waste batteries to a recycling company. For housekeeping, the main issue is the control of detergent dose so we use the detergent dose dispenser provided by Ecolab, our detergent supplier. Also, we have a green tip board located at the staff canteen. There are many ideas that we share with all employees there.

Ecolab[2] provides training and technical support to Fairmont housekeeping staff concerning detergent usage and guidance for the effective application of certain detergents to different cleaning tasks. Ecolab also checks that staff use the detergents in the right way. Emily Liu explains: "For example, three sprays are needed to clean a bathtub. Some cleaners may think it is not a big deal if he or she sprays more times than required. But if a housekeeper sprays ten times, it is a waste." If necessary, Ecolab provides additional training on how to use products in an environmentally friendly way. As Emily Liu says, "When we work with Ecolab, we learn from them. They know their detergents and the right way to achieve the best results with the least possible dose."

Employees at Fairmont in China have come up with many ideas of their own, including educational programmes introducing environmental issues to guests, organic farming and delivering organic vegetables to guests' homes (of which more below). As well as complex engineering solutions for saving energy, they also come up with simple ideas such as stopping the use of paper cups. Fairmont people will never use disposable cups as these are wasteful and their use is "the wrong thing to do".

Fairmont employees also look after each other. If someone forgets to turn off the lights or the water tap a colleague will remind them. For example, security departments use a checklist when doing the rounds every night to report if lights or heat have been turned off or left on. The security report is always discussed as part of the morning briefing. Fairmont employees know they must remember

---

2   Ecolab is a global company that works with a number of hotels in the industry in China. Ecolab provides safe and effective products that have a positive impact on people and the environment. Ecolab detergents address national standards in the ingredients of chemicals and disinfectants.

to turn off the lights or they will hear about it at the briefing next morning.

This culture begins from the moment employees join the company. Sannie Sun, Learning and Development Manager at Fairmont Yangcheng Lake, says:

> we have orientation training for new staff during the first week. After they are assigned to their departments they receive a copy of the action plan and job task checklist, which includes the knowledge they need to grasp for their job. In the checklist, there is a section called "doing". This includes green projects, representation in the green committee and responsible requirements of the hotel.

Flora Li, Director of Housekeeping, feels the importance of these programmes very strongly:

> I feel that people don't receive enough education on this. They should be told the harmful consequences of their actions. China hasn't developed enough to pay much attention to these problems. Most Chinese people's priority is how to become more affluent rather than environmental protection. It is an issue of mind-set change. We educate our employees on how to reduce the use of water. The practice is applicable not only to their jobs but to their personal daily life, which has much more impact on society.

1.4 Strengthening commitments

Globally, in nearly all hotels it is now standard practice for guests to put their room cards into slots next to the doors (or main switch) to run electricity. In some hotels guests (or even housekeepers) leave extra keys in the slot to keep the air conditioning running non-stop, even if they are not in the room. Fairmont does not use this system, as it is not eco-friendly. Instead, motion sensors detect when a guest enters the room and switches on the required lights along with the air conditioning in the required position. When guests leave the room, the air conditioning switches off automatically.

Fairmont also uses environmentally friendly technology in its bathrooms. The technique is called "rain forest" and it is based on pressurizing the shower heads. The amount of water coming from the shower resembles a mist, covering a large area and providing the feeling of a large amount of water but with a soft touch approach.

On average, each guest produces over 2 pounds (1 kg) of waste each night, mostly composed of beverage and paper products. These account for 65% of all hotel waste. As well as ordinary refuse bins, Fairmont hotels provide a separate bin for recycling so that if guests do want to recycle they have that option. "We give the guests in each room an option of a recycle bin, which you might not find in many other hotels globally," says Emily Liu. "This is how we collaborate with our customers." There are also intensive back-of-the-house efforts to recycle a number of products as well as organics diversions from the hotels' kitchens.

Fairmont's waste management programme has three separate strands:

1. Implementation of comprehensive recycling programmes

2. Organics and composting programmes to capture food waste from kitchens

3. Redistribution of untouched food, partially used amenities and household goods to local groups and shelters

In the spirit of "think globally and act locally", ongoing sustainability projects are tailored to each property. This concept was launched in January 2005 as one of the latest additions to Fairmont's Green Partnership programme.

However, it can be hard to tell whether local producers use non-organic fertilizers or pesticides to produce food. At present, traceability in China is based mostly on trust.

Laundry is a particularly important issue because of the health implications. Flora Li notes that when choosing a laundry service supplier for the Fairmont Beijing, Fairmont managers went to visit the supplier's premises. "They had to show us all their written documents such as qualifications, certification and the inspection report of the epidemic prevention station," she says. At Yangcheng Lake, Fairmont has its own laundry which also provides services for other hotels in the area. Fairmont laundry machines are highly sophisticated and have high standards for water and energy saving. As Sannie Sun says, "Our market investigations found that hotels tend to outsource their laundry. Our hotel has the capacity to take in laundry, and we make good profits out of this business."

1.5 Responsible purchasing and local organic trust

Local sourcing is a key part of Fairmont's philosophy. Fairmont recognizes the importance of its business to local communities, especially in terms of local purchasing, and strives wherever possible to purchase local products and to help the economies of the communities where it does business. In China, Fairmont also collaborates with suppliers to help reduce their CO_2 emissions. For example, Fairmont is trying to work with suppliers who use recycled paper, even to produce business cards. As Reto Boer, Director of Food and Beverages at the Fairmont Beijing, says, "we are very careful about what and from where we purchase. We have strategic partnerships with companies outside and within China but the key point (for supplier selection) is that we focus on the green standards of the suppliers."

Wherever any hotel in the Fairmont network can find green suppliers, then those green suppliers are given preference. Fairmont buys organic food because it believes it is the right thing to do. Organic food is of course more expensive, but this is what Fairmont guests are looking for and expecting. Fairmont restaurants will not put certain things such as bluefin tuna or shark's fin on the menu as these are endangered species. Fairmont suppliers are also aware that Fairmont will not buy endangered food even if it is available. In most cases the chefs control the food supplies because "we feel that a chef knows more about food than a manager does". In doing so, "chefs try to find things close to home instead of going out there in the world," says Reto Boer.

Fairmont has found a number of organic suppliers around Beijing – including on a golf course that has a few greenhouses. "We searched for the green producers, we approached them and we said we want to buy organic food, and they plant for us what we need." Fairmont makes inspections and checks to make sure that green producers follow the standards to avoid "cheating". "We try to get as much as possible from the local market because we don't believe in flying everywhere to all parts of the world and increasing the carbon footprint," says Reto Boer. "We even provide our guests with bicycles to use free of charge as part of the sustainability programme."

When Fairmont first began operations in China it asked all hotel employees how important it is for them to have to work in a green hotel. Ninety-five per cent of the staff responded that it is "very, very important". When asked why, one of the things that came up was river fish. People cannot eat river fish any more in China because the rivers are polluted. Staff identified this as an issue they wished to do something about. For a start, Fairmont is very careful about how it sources its fish. It will sometimes import fish which it knows have been farmed in a responsible manner, rather than using local fish, which may have been fished using unsustainable practices or from polluted water. This may seem to go against the principle of local sourcing, but this is one of several trade-offs that Fairmont has found it has to make in order to follow its core principles.

1.6 Eco-cuisine

Mohammad Kuhi, Executive Chef at the Fairmont Yangcheng Lake Fairmont, says that:

> there is no other hotel in the world right now that can afford to have a farm on-site to produce all its own beautiful vegetables. There are some small-scale farms, but ours is enormous, has all the resources we need and is expanding. At the moment we are building a huge greenhouse.

Today Fairmont Yangcheng Lake Farm provides nearly 75% of vegetable supplies to the hotel and partly supplies the Peace hotel in Shanghai.

Yangcheng Lake Farm is owned by the Kunshan city government and managed by Fairmont, which grows everything from seasonal vegetables popular in Shanghai to Western herbs. Fairmont buys 80% of food locally, within a radius of approximately 20 miles. Chicken, duck and pork are supplied locally from Kunshan or Suzhou. When Fairmont is unable to get the best-quality meat locally it looks for the best possible source; lamb, for example, is sourced from Mongolia.

There are not many organic meat producers in China, and Fairmont has had difficulty in sourcing organic chicken or duck. Traceability is highly important. Chef Mohammad Kuhi wants to be sure that the chicken is organically farmed, so he visits the farms to check. If their chickens are organically reared according to Fairmont standards he will buy them all.

The philosophy of buying locally is very strong at Fairmont Yangcheng Lake, and the company encourages its chefs to buy local produce whenever possible. As Chef Mohammad Kuhi points out, "at Fairmont we want to showcase the local, authentic food". Imported vegetables are more expensive and more perishable. Food delivered from a long distance is a waste of taste and a loss of money.

The hotel farm is run by the executive chef, who tells the farm managers what seasonal vegetables the kitchen needs, and then the farm grows them. It was not built to make profit, but for the benefit of the guests so they could enjoy the real taste of organic food. The farm has made a deep impression on guests at the Fairmont Yangcheng Lake. Some of the guests who come to the hotel choose it for the organic food and the farm. For many, arriving to stay for the weekend or on holiday from Shanghai, a visit to the farm is the first thing they do after checking in. When guests go to dinner at the hotel, they can choose three vegetables from the farm to be cooked on-site and they can also take home up to 3 kg of vegetables free, as a gift from the hotel. Fairmont offers this service as part of a new "Spring Package". A client can get a room, two breakfasts, recreation activities, a credit towards other food and beverages and a box of vegetables to take home. Philip Smith says, "It is very common that on a Friday and a Saturday night we have 100% occupancy, and sometimes on weekdays we get that as well."

At the entrance to the restaurant there is always a display of local organic vegetables. When a guest walks in he or she can choose the vegetables the chef will cook with. The chef then uses his creativity to make a six-course menu with vegetables all wok-fried. The guests choose the style, Western or Chinese. The difference lies not in raw materials but in the cooking methods. Western-friendly cuisine requires less oil while Chinese recipes have more bok choi and are oily. In Mohammed Kuhi's view, "this experience, what we're trying to provide now, one doesn't get anywhere. It is a unique food experience, an innovative model based on organic luxury, customers' learning and no boundaries, as the menu is not fixed".

The farm is partly subsidized by the Kunshan local government. The hotel pays a fixed rate for the labour costs and the farmers are workers employed by the government.[3] The government does not intend to make a profit either. Instead the farm is part of Kunshan's master plan to keep Yangcheng Lake free from pesticides and to create a source of healthy real food, and so promote chemical-free eating. Thus whatever vegetables are produced, the labour costs to Fairmont do not change and are much lower than the market price.

Fairmont chefs spend a great deal of time doing market surveys to ensure that they are getting the best prices. The executive chef sends his team to check on local prices three times per week, to get to know what they can get around the region and make price comparisons. For example, when the bean sprout is in season and executive chefs wants to put it on the menu, chefs go and speak to farmers to learn when exactly they will harvest. This is crucial as the weather might cause some delays or unusual warmth might bring the harvest on early. Chefs at the Yangcheng Lake Hotel also learn about rice cultivation. Chef Mohammad Kuhi explains:

> last year we had our first harvest – we got beautiful white and brown rice. This year we'll harvest more because we have learned. It was a test – we planted the rice to see how it grows. We managed to get only 70% of the rice, the rest dried up, there was not enough water and the sun was too strong. This

3   The workers are employed by the state-owned Kunshan City Investment Company (KCID). Fairmont Yangcheng Lake is operated and owned by KCID, which also owns the water park and the farm as part of the same property.

> year we will probably get 100% of the crop. So it's all a learn-
> ing process. It's great when the farm is new because you are
> learning, you are trying, testing and you know more.

In line with staff priorities, above, Fairmont is also looking at the idea of building a fish farm. Kunshan used to be a fishing village, but at present the water is contaminated by refuse. Fairmont wants to start a project to clear and clean a small waterway, replanting vegetation that is native to it. Fairmont then plans to restock the cleaned waterway with fish. Many people in Kunshan still want to make a living by fishing, and Fairmont's desire is to give something back to the community as well as doing something good for the environment.

Fairmont Yangcheng Lake guests are aware that it is a standard practice not only for the chefs to go every day to the farm to get vegetables for cooking but also for the farmers to go to the kitchen every day to collect natural waste. All uncooked vegetable trimmings and cuttings are sent back to the farm for composting. Cooked waste goes to the pig farm – a contractor comes to Fairmont to separate this waste. Oil and plastic waste, paper boxes and so on are collected weekly by a recycling company from a special garbage room.

Philip Smith makes a comparative overview of the composting and recycling systems:

> In China we actually get paid for our garbage whereas in
> North America you separate all your products and then you
> would pay someone to take garbage away. Here we have one
> person that picks up all of our garbage and sorts it all: glass,
> paper, cans, and food scraps going out to composting or to pig
> farms. They pick up all of our garbage and they actually give
> me a monthly income for the rubbish. So you've actually found
> a very interesting way of looking at it because these people
> want to make money off our garbage. If there is anything out
> of the garbage that can be sold, in China it is sold.

There are four operators in the recycling chain in the area with whom Fairmont can cooperate. The operators come to Fairmont and give quotes. As Philip Smith says:

> I used to pay tens of thousands of dollars per month for garbage hauling or dumping things at a refuse dump. Here the operators will actually bid and say OK I will give you RMB 10,000 per month for your garbage, and they do it based on that premise that they will take the garbage away, sort through it at their facilities and sell whatever can be recycled. Very little goes to the landfill, only something that truly cannot be processed.

As noted above, food scraps and organic waste are sent back to the farm for composting locally. To ease transportation, the hotel uses a special machine that dries the food waste.

Fairmont hopes that others will observe their environmental efforts and that this will start to generate a broader sense of responsibility. Local people might stop putting refuse into the waterways, for example. Fairmont also believes that other companies will follow its example. There are many foreign companies in Kunshan, and if every company picks one waterway and spends the money and time to clean up and rejuvenate it, this will make an impact on Kunshan's sustainability. Fairmont wants to show that the hotel is not just a business: it can have an impact in many other ways.

1.7 Culture and values

Seasonal harvesting has become a major attraction for Fairmont at Yangcheng Lake. At the lotus harvest time, for example, people will come to pick their own lotus roots. "In the supermarket you can get the lotus root already washed and cleaned up," says Philip Smith. "But people prefer it fresh here, from the earth with all little strings hanging off the sides. They take it home and email us back saying, 'we cooked the lotus root – it's the best lotus root we ever had'." The water chestnut harvest is also very popular. Mid-September to mid-December is another popular time as this is when the hairy crabs are in season.[4] "Hairy crabs are famous throughout Asia," says Smith, "and people want to come and try the crab during those three months because that's when they are at their best. You can still buy a crab out of season but they are not the same quality as during those months." In these and other ways Fairmont helps to reintroduce people to the environment.

"A lot of people come out here and are really thrilled to be able to bring their kids," says Philip Smith. "When they were kids themselves they used to go fishing around the Shanghai area. Now, Fairmont Yangcheng Lake Resort is the place to come for Chinese for fishing with their children." The price for fishing is cheap, 50 yuan for four hours. Fairmont also offers cormorant fishing, and Chinese tea the way it was done in the "old days", which these days is something unique. Philip Smith continues:

> In the Tahoe lake area, about half an hour away there is a lady, a hotel employee, who keeps a tea farm on Lake Tahoe. It is her original home and she makes tea for us and takes care of the place. On the tea farm there are as many as 24 beehives which

4   Hairy crabs are dark-green crustaceans with wispy brown "fur" on their claws. They are prized for their roe and oil, which turns a brilliant orange hue when cooked and is exceptionally rich. "The best crabs come from Yangcheng Lake in Suzhou, in the Jiangsu Province near Shanghai. The season starts in September, when female crabs are best, and continues through the end of the year, with male crabs offering the most succulent roe from mid-October on" (McMillan, A.F. (2010, October 19). Where to find an autumn seafood special in Hong Kong. *The New York Times*. Retrieved from http://intransit.blogs.nytimes.com/2010/10/19/where-to-find-an-autumn-seafood-special-in-hong-kong/).

produce in spring around 30 to 50 litres of organic honey daily. Fairmont uses this honey for cooking and desserts.

Old traditions are applied not only to the tea ceremonies but to construction as well. "A lot of people don't realize how much hard work it was to build the farm," says Philip Smith. "There's not a single nail [in the construction], it's all made with wood, all is done in the traditional way going back to a couple of hundred years ago." For the farm Fairmont used special woven material based on tartar to build the farmhouse. This is part of the programme of preserving local culture and craftsmanship. In a similar fashion, in Beijing, Fairmont is collaborating with the Beijing Cultural Heritage Protection Centre to organize trips for guests who can go to a real hutong and see what life in the city used to be like. "We give them the option to donate some money so that this organization will continue to exist and do good work to preserve the original Beijing, instead of getting another skyscraper city which nobody really needs," says Hans Hordijk. Fairmont also provides financial support to the China Association for Preservation Technology of Cultural Relics and WWF to protect the hutongs in Beijing.

At Yangcheng Lake, says Philip Smith, there are further plans. "We want to have 60 to 70 valleys in this area and recreate traditional old-style water villages." Guests will travel to the valleys by boat and:

> see what the life was like. Our thinking is not only about green farming, healthy food and fishing in the lake making for a "great restaurant" but is also about experiential learning to reintroduce the history and culture that China has to offer. China has some of the most ancient culture and history in the world. It is great to introduce people to that history as much as possible.

Through leisure Fairmont is trying to change the behaviour of customers towards the environment. Owen Fu, Director of Recreation at Fairmont Yangcheng Lake, provides an example:

> We created a programme for the kids to understand how to protect the ecosystem here at Yangcheng Lake. We explain the negative consequences of dumping cigarette ends into the lake. We also provide learning sessions called "Kids Discovery". We show them something they can never learn in the city. We present, for example, a waterwheel and tell a story about how the fields were irrigated traditionally. We teach them how water is recycled in a traditional community without too much waste. What is the cultural background, mechanical principles involved and effects that irrigation can produce?

This is an exploratory process for children and cultivates habits of protecting the environment, understanding the importance of the ecosystem equilibrium while playing and enjoying. The director of recreation intends to set up a Fairmont Discovery School and give children T-shirts with the school logo. He hopes that the sense of belonging to a discovery community might raise interest in other children who see the T-shirt and want to come to the Fairmont hotel to play.

Fairmont also brings its products to the homes of customers, an idea that seems to have been unknown in the hotel industry until now. For around RMB 3,500 per month, people living in the area of Kunshan can get up to 5 kg of organic vegetables per week delivered to their door. Fairmont is looking to expand this programme into the Shanghai area. As Philip Smith explains:

> some of our hotel guests who want to buy from the farm – they asked us if they could take our vegetables home with them. So we want to be able to say, "Great! Please subscribe and we'll send weekly vegetables to your home."

1.8 Social responsibility efforts

In another venture, Fairmont has started to work with children with Down's syndrome. In China the government usually looks after children with Down's syndrome until they are 14; then they are sent back to their families. Many do not get to play an active part in society. People with disabilities in China often have fewer opportunities than the general population. Of the 19 to 21 million such people in China, only 7.1% have meaningful employment.[5] In Beijing there is a special commune, Te Ao Farm, which tries to better integrate people with intellectual disabilities into society by providing work for them in orchards or helping farmers. Fairmont buys fruit (apples, pears, peaches and apricots) from the farm to support the workers in their desire to contribute to society. Fairmont is considering, as a next step, bringing in a few children for a year of training, for example, learning the basics in housekeeping or preparatory work in the kitchen with the aim of getting a job at the hotel. Fairmont is looking forward to "making an impact and helping people with intellectual disabilities to live more independent lives and have a feeling of being responsible and useful to the community," says Reto Borer.

Fairmont is currently the only hotel that buys from the special commune. The commune does not have an organic certificate, but Fairmont chefs have visited the place many times to ensure that they follow organic standards as closely as possible. Fairmont has good relationships with the farm's founder and teachers, and trusts them to ensure that the food is produced organically. Fairmont buys, for

5   Li, J., Li, J., Huang, Y., & Thornicroft, G. (2014). Mental health training program for community mental health staff in Guangzhou, China: effects on knowledge of mental illness and stigma. *International Journal of Mental Health Systems*, 8(49).

example, 100 kg of cucumbers a week to support the farm, and this money is reinvested into the school. Fairmont managers visit the commune several times a year to see the progress at the school, examine the dormitory, and check that the houses are painted and the grounds are maintained as a part of their charity activities.

At the beginning of 2012 Fairmont started a cooperation project with small farms situtated around the special commune outside of Beijing. Fairmont offered the farmers a business model based on organic farming and employing students from the special commune. Today, fruits and vegetables including apples, oranges, peaches, cucumbers, pumpkins and tomatoes are bought from eight of these small farms, each of which is committed to hiring at least one student. These farms supply about 70% of the Fairmont Beijing's requirements, and Fairmont pays about 3% higher than market rates in order to support the commune.

With the assistance of a job trainer, Fairmont hopes to help students from the special commune feel more empowered. As Reto Borer says, "they have their dreams, aspirations, and wishes for themselves and their families. If Fairmont can make a difference here, then that is corporate social responsibility." At Fairmont Beijing, uniquely for any hotel in China, there are already three employees with learning disabilities.

1.9 The final word

Fairmont is a strong believer in local sourcing but this philosophy is sometimes sacrificed when quality might be compromised. Responsible shipping and sustainable production are issues Fairmont is confronted with daily when sourcing in China. As Reto Borer says:

> I am fully aware that I increase the carbon footprint when things have to be flown or shipped in, but organic food is a big problem for us in China. Sometimes we have to ship salmon from Norway because we know the Norwegian farmer is controlled by the European government [*sic*] and has a responsible management system in place. We are aware that we increase the carbon footprint by bringing that salmon from Norway instead of Vietnam or Chile, which would also be half the price. We don't do that because recently we learned that Chilean salmon, for example, had a very high toxin value. As a result they reduced farming by half.

Sourcing local produce has its own challenges: some local farms will provide certificates if asked, but it can be hard to tell whether these are genuine. In 2011 Fairmont Shanghai learned this the hard way when the hotel received a weekly delivery of oysters from Canada in a basket covered with a mesh, sealed by the Canadian export authority and customs office. One of the batches was of poor quality and there was a serious case of food poisoning. As part of the subsequent investigation Fairmont sent the oysters to a lab for testing. The lab report showed that the water remaining in the oysters was not of Canadian origin, but came from southern China. Though Fairmont received the supply with the original documentation, apparently sealed by the Canadian export authority, in reality the oysters came from China. Further investigation showed that the seal was a forgery.

Another problem concerns overpopulation and food supply, an especially urgent problem for China. Many farmers use chemicals such as pesticides and fertilizers in China as a way to try to increase production. On the one hand many Chinese people are still hungry; but on the other hand many are becoming more affluent. Increasingly a Chinese family can afford meat or fish every day. This demand is satisfied by producing more pork, more chicken and more fish – and more quickly – than was the case 15 years ago. For example, farmers feed pigs with hormones so that they will grow faster. Such meat can cause health issues in humans, but this is seen as a way to satisfy demand for food in China.[6] From a sustainability perspective, it is difficult to balance the need for a supply of healthy food with a billion people demanding, "I want to eat meat tonight."

Flora Li, Head of Housekeeping at the Fairmont Beijing, believes that the educational background of employees and lack of general environmental awareness compound the problem:

> We are trying our best to educate our employees not to use chemical detergents at both hotel and home every day. If chemical detergents were used every day, a significant amount of sewage would be produced. In the future, environmental pollution will be a big problem, and that is why we educate our employees about environmental protection. The average staff education level in the hospitality industry is not high. We know what environmental protection is, and its significance for future generations. But our staff do not yet have this awareness.

Another challenge is the affordability of such initiatives for the average consumer. Fairmont is a luxury hotel chain, with typical room rates charged at above RMB 2,000 per night for a standard room. There is a decision to be made with regard to the trade-off between profitability/cost efficiency, environmental and social sustainability and customer experience.

When we asked Fairmont what lessons they had learned from their sustainable innovations, the answer was very simple: "By spending a little bit of money you can save a lot more. We have programmes in place that other hotel companies can only dream of."

---

6   Schneider, M. (2011). Feeding China's pigs: implications for the environment, China's smallholder farmers and food security. *Institute for Agriculture and Trade Policy*, May 2011.

1.10 Case summary

Fairmont is the world's first hotel chain to operate in a socially and environmentally responsible fashion, and this has contributed to the company's success. Social and environmental responsibility have helped to create strong customer relationships and add value for both the hotel operator and its guests. In this case we looked at Fairmont's operations generally, but focused in particular on the innovative projects carried out at the Fairmont Yangcheng Lake Hotel near Shanghai. Key features of Fairmont's programme include:

- Energy conservation programmes, reducing consumption of gas and also of water

- Reducing waste, recycling kitchen waste and reducing packaging

- Setting up "green committees" to give staff a voice on how to implement sustainable solutions, and also to come up with solutions of their own

- Collaboration with suppliers to reduce CO_2 emissions

- Using locally and/or organically sourced ingredients wherever possible in restaurant kitchens: for example, the farm at Yangcheng Lake which supplies all the hotel's vegetables

- Recognizing the importance of local communities and contributing to their economies wherever Fairmont operates

2
Learning to be sustainable: Hewlett-Packard

2.1 Introduction

Hewlett-Packard Company, commonly referred to as HP, is an American multinational information technology corporation headquartered in Palo Alto, California. The company was founded by Bill Hewlett and Dave Packard, who both graduated in electrical engineering from Stanford University in 1935. Bill and Dave established their company in 1939 in a one-car garage, with an initial capital investment of US$538. They tossed a coin to decide whether the company would be called Hewlett-Packard or Packard-Hewlett. Today Hewlett-Packard is known as the world's leading information technology company with major product lines including personal computing devices, industry standard servers, related storage devices, networking products, software, IT services and a diverse range of printers. HP specializes in developing and manufacturing computing, data storage, and networking hardware, designing software and delivering services.

In September 2009, Newsweek ranked HP first in its 2009 Green Rankings of America's 500 largest corporations. According to Environmental Leader:

> Hewlett-Packard earned its number one position due to its greenhouse gas (GHG) emission reduction programmes, and was the first major IT-company to report GHG emissions associated with its supply chain, according to the ranking. In addition, HP has made an effort to remove toxic substances from its products, though Greenpeace has targeted the company for not doing better.[1]

In 2013 HP published its complete carbon footprint, making it among the first companies globally to disclose this level of information.

HP emphasizes a holistic approach to sustainability at each stage of the product or service life-cycle. It has introduced innovations in PC and printer products, as well as data centre services. As the world's largest provider of IT infrastructure, software, services and solutions to individuals and organizations of all sizes, HP is in a unique position to help customers turn energy consumption data into usable information, enabling them to develop more efficient and productive operations that use less energy and reduce associated GHG emissions. HP is also committed to improving energy efficiency across its portfolio of products, from desktop PCs and printers to data centres.

HP joined the WWF Climate Savers programme in 2008, achieved the goal of reducing GHG emissions by 20% in 2010 compared with its 2005 level, and made a further commitment to reduce GHG emissions by 20% compared with its 2010 level by 2020. WWF commended HP for its strong commitment to energy reduction – not only for reducing GHG emissions within its own operations

---

1   See http://www.environmentalleader.com/2009/09/22/hp.

and supply chain, but for placing a strong emphasis on increasing energy efficiency in its products.

This case study focuses on the environmental sustainability practices of HP in China. More specifically, it attempts to discover how HP creates a green supply chain (upstream and downstream) in China. HP's green supply chain has been achieved through the following strategies:

- Use of advanced technologies (e.g. data centres) and services to help customers reduce CO_2 emissions

- Reduction of suppliers' GHG emissions through energy efficiency training and development

2.2 HP China: an overview

HP opened its first office in Beijing in 1981. HP China was established in 1985, and manufacturing operations commenced in Shanghai in 1995. HP's Printing and Personal Systems Group opened the China Development Centre in Shanghai in 2004 to design and manufacture products specifically for the Chinese market. The first HP China Lab opened in 2005, focusing on networking and communications.

By 2013 HP was the second-largest PC maker in the world, and the leading foreign PC vendor in China according to the International Data Corporation (IDC). HP China now has its main operations in Shanghai, Chongqing and Tianjin, with its headquarters in Beijing. A second factory was built in western China, Chongqing, in 2008. This 20,000 m^2 factory was constructed to produce notebooks and desktop computers for sale within China, and to compete with Lenovo. "The establishment of the new plant will accelerate our expansion in the region," explained Isaiah Cheung, Vice President of HP China, in a press release. In April 2012, HP signed an agreement to work with partners to set up a new manufacturing facility in Chongqing. This facility produces ink-jet printers, laser printers and ink cartridges.

HP's move to Chongqing was not only strategically important for the company but also turned out to be significant for the city. Chongqing is traditionally home to heavy industrial production such as shipbuilding, metallurgy, automotive manufacturing, and defence and precision instruments. Today IT manufacturing has become another pillar of local industry and the city supports many suppliers to big electronics original equipment manufacturers (OEMs). In addition to the manufacturing of printers and laptops, HP brought packaging and logistics suppliers to Chongqing. The city has since become one of HP's global procurement centres. An international rail freight network linking China to Europe from Chongqing has already been built. This logistics arrangement has already significantly reduced the carbon emissions of intermodal shipments by road and sea. In addition, many migrant workers from the region no longer need to move to coastal cities for jobs, as they can now find employment close to their home.

Production, however, is not the only matter concerning HP. As early as 2005, it organized the first supplier Social and Environmental Responsibility (SER) forum in China. More than 330 representatives of regional Chinese suppliers came to discuss the HP Corporate Social Responsibility (CSR) strategy, including HP's policy on the Restriction of Hazardous Substances.

In 2010, HP China's environmental sustainability efforts increased when it became the only IT company to join the Energy Efficiency Programme (EEP), a year-long pilot programme designed to help major suppliers in China reduce energy use and GHG emissions. Through the EEP, suppliers can save costs through more efficient energy usage. HP worked directly with suppliers to share knowledge and best practices in order to help suppliers create energy efficiency projects.

2.3 Reduction of GHG emissions for corporate customers

As the world's largest provider of IT infrastructure, software, services and solutions to individuals and organizations of all sizes, HP is in a position to help customers turn energy consumption data into usable information, thus enabling them to develop more efficient and productive operations that use less energy and reduce associated GHG emissions. For example:

- HP Energy and Sustainability Management (ESM) is a service business designed to help enterprise customers measure and manage energy use and other resources across their facilities, IT, supply chain and workforce. ESM advised the Chongqing city government on technology and software solutions best suited to reduce its energy use, decrease GHG emissions and meet established goals. The project included a rapid assessment of the city's ongoing energy use to identify opportunities to reduce a growing energy budget.

- HP has developed a Cloud Sustainability Dashboard (CSD) to help IT professionals better understand and quantify the sustainability impact of cloud computing. The dashboard provides a high-level view of the economic, environmental and social impacts of related IT and facility resources and services, including servers, storage, networking, power, cooling and IT support.

- HP "Thin Clients" enable computing on a "virtual desktop" residing on a central server. Users access the virtual environment through a simple and efficient desktop device that contains no hard drives or other moving parts, relying on the server for all computing resources. A company replacing 2,000 desktop PCs and monitors, made in 2005, with the same number of HP thin client solutions – including the required servers – would cut energy consumption by 74% and save an estimated 795,000 kilowatt hours (kWh) per year.

- HP Smart Grid Solutions enables utility companies and other partners to design and deploy dynamic pricing programmes and energy efficiency, conservation and demand–response programmes. With operational improvements, utility companies can limit outages and develop business plans that can defer the build-out of new generation and transmission infrastructure.

2.3.1 Energy-efficient data centres

Data centre services include comprehensive networking, storage and server assessment; energy efficiency evaluation; and data centre design and management. The latest HP ProLiant G7 and Gen8 servers are ENERGY STAR[2] qualified, helping customers reduce energy consumption, reclaim capacity and extend the life of the data centre.

2   ENERGY STAR is a voluntary energy efficiency programme sponsored by the US Environmental Protection Agency. Many models of HP office products are ENERGY STAR certified.

Another service business, HP Critical Facilities Services (CFS), provides strategic consulting, design, building and operational assurance resources to help customers upgrade existing data centres or build more efficient new facilities. One solution on offer is the HP Flexible Data Center, which uses prefabricated, standardized components to shorten the time it takes to build and deploy a data centre. In addition to lower capital costs and a quicker time to market, HP Flexible Data Center configurations improve the use of power and cooling resources to reduce energy and water consumption, and decrease GHG emissions. The Flexible Data Center can cut energy costs by nearly 14% and reduce the annualized power usage effectiveness (PUE) rating by 13.2%, compared with a traditional data centre. Furthermore, HP CFS helps customers achieve key energy efficiency certifications such as the US Green Building Council (USGBC) LEED Standard for Data Centres, US Environmental Protection Agency (EPA) ENERGY STAR for Data Centres, and US Department of Energy (DOE) "Save Energy Now". As of April 2012, HP CFS had designed more than 60% of all LEED-certified data centres.

2.3.2 HP helps Volkswagen China transform its data centre

Volkswagen was one of the first international automotive manufacturers to set up operations in China, entering the market in 1984. Today it has 14 divisions across the country, including manufacturing, spare parts and servicing. The single data centre that provided infrastructure services for the entire Volkswagen Group in China was in desperate need of an upgrade. Most urgently, there was no effective integrated automated monitoring system, the air-conditioning and alarm systems were faulty, the network wiring needed attention, and there were serious power supply hazards.

Aware that it needed to fix these reliability issues to deliver a highly scalable, flexible alternative, the Volkswagen Group met with several vendors. It selected the CFS team from HP Technology Services to complete the online upgrade and transformation of the data centre.

The transformation process took more than six months. The HP CFS team successfully optimized and transformed Volkswagen Group China's power distribution organization, reorganized the cooling system and air circulation, segregated and transformed the IT function areas, migrated the entire network structure, set up a new wiring system, and adjusted the layout of the core applications. It also improved and integrated the overall infrastructure monitoring methods of the data centre.

Since its transformation, Volkswagen Group China's data centre has not experienced any downtime, and the data centre is saving energy. The power usage effectiveness (PUE) value went from more than 2.5 prior to the transformation to 1.8, helping Volkswagen Group China use 30–40% less power. With a new layout and repositioning of the equipment, there is now almost 50% more space in the data centre. The data centre previously housed 30 cabinets in three rows; now it houses 50 cabinets in five rows, adding significant scalability to the system. In addition, HP installed a dynamic environment monitoring system in the data centre to report abnormalities in the main server room power distribution, main equipment, cabinets, temperature and humidity.

2.4 GHG emission reduction in HP's supply chain

HP's experience in China shows that the primary barrier to working with suppliers on GHG emission reduction involves supplier commitment to invest in energy savings. Levels of commitment can vary from company to company. Managers of state-owned companies, having struggled for survival throughout the 1990s, find it difficult to justify the long-term investment needed for creating energy savings. Short-term returns tend to dominate investment decisions. Shareholders, on the other hand, tend to be more willing to invest in sustainability to improve environmental performance and brand image.

Putting ownership aside, however, HP feels it is important to engage with suppliers at different levels of management – general managers, middle managers, business groups, and those in charge of energy efficiency – to communicate a consistent message and achieve a strong commitment from suppliers with regard to energy savings.

To ensure adequate communication and a consistent message, HP meets regularly with suppliers to discuss not only quality and innovation, but also the corporate social responsibility (CSR) strategy of the suppliers. Interestingly, HP has noticed that those suppliers who are more engaged in its SER programme enjoy better overall performance.

Cost-effectiveness is not the only thing driving companies to lower energy use. All Chinese companies are required to follow the national policy of the 12th Five-Year Plan, which calls for them to reduce GHG emissions. Saving energy is one way to "pick the low-hanging fruit".[3] The best companies see this as an opportunity to employ new core technology and/or new business models. For example, one HP supplier changed its manufacturing process by improving the design of a battery and changing the raw materials

3   China's 12th Five-Year Plan (2011–15): full English version at http://cbi.typepad.com/china_direct/2011/05/chinas-twelfth-five-new-plan-the-full-english-version.html.

that went into the battery, as a way to extend the battery life. These kinds of supplier intentionally incorporate green design and green materials into their research and development (R&D) processes. It is important to note that supplier R&D efforts can be managed alongside HP's procurement management procedures and in communication with the sourcing team.

Because of its vast market presence, HP is in a position to monitor emerging customer requirements, and to match these with opportunities for new green materials and innovative green designs within its vast supplier community. Interactions with the HP purchasing team enable suppliers to stay abreast of updated material compliance and the requirements of energy efficiency, eco-labelling and green design. The overall strategy is to translate concepts into product design, merchandising, procurement practices and manufacturing so as to influence the greening of the supply chain.

2.4.1 The Energy Efficiency Programme (EEP)

Ernest Wong, HP's Asia–Pacific Social and Environmental Responsibility Supply Chain Manager, is responsible for the implementation of social and environmental responsibility initiatives for the hardware products at HP China. He explains that, "HP is the first company in the electronics industry to publicly disclose its supply chain carbon footprint. We would like to extend support to help suppliers on energy-saving efforts and to develop the EEP programme."

HP's understanding of supply chain carbon footprint management came gradually, mostly through learning by doing. Having gained some knowledge from inside the company itself, HP realized that it is essential to look at suppliers' carbon footprints and search for energy reduction opportunities within the supply chain. HP helped lead the development of an industry-wide carbon and energy data collection system together with the Electronic Industry

Citizenship Coalition (EICC) in 2007, and successfully collected carbon-related information from 81% of its suppliers by spend in 2008.

By mid-2010 HP had joined Business for Social Responsibility (BSR) – a nonprofit organization that supports members' sustainability initiatives – in their Energy Efficiency Partnership Programme, that helps suppliers improve energy management practices and to share best practice. HP also invited 12 of its suppliers to join the programme. As well as providing training, quarterly meetings and technical consultations such as energy audits, the suppliers also submitted action plans around energy management, resulting in 24 new energy-saving projects. Because energy efficiency initiatives are more voluntary than mandatory, HP has expended much effort to convince Chinese suppliers to join the Energy Efficiency Partnership Programme.

The IT industry supply base consists of several layers, or tiers. HP has first-tier suppliers – suppliers who directly supply HP and therefore can work directly with HP on energy-saving opportunities. But key suppliers have their own suppliers, the so-called sub-tiers. The issue is how all the parties – Tier 1 suppliers, Tier 2 suppliers and beyond – can work together.

HP summarized what it learned through the Energy Efficiency Partnership Programme and identified best practices around technical feasibility, broad applicability, investment payback period and significance. The findings were shared with the suppliers who took part in the Energy Efficiency Partnership Programme. Further energy-saving technologies specific to production, such as injection moulding, were also addressed.

2.4.2 Implementing the Energy Efficiency Programme

Implementing the EEP requires cross-company collaboration, beyond simple customer/supplier contract negotiations. In order to create the conditions for collaborative innovation, HP has worked with partners such as BSR, WWF Hong Kong and other energy service companies (ESCOs). With BSR's help, HP trained 12 Tier 1 suppliers in 2010. It has worked with WWF HK since 2011 for a new round of EEP, training an additional 35 Tier 1 suppliers. As a next step, HP intends to focus more attention on promoting energy savings deeper into the supply chain upstream of Tier 1, and on training sub-tier suppliers.

Through working groups across several industries, BSR is helping manufacturers reduce their energy use and associated GHG emissions, as well as lower overall energy costs. Fengyuan Wang, a Manager of Advisory Services at BSR Hong Kong, said: "HP has been very active in the Energy Efficiency Partnership Programme project, and during the past two years we have made great achievements together." BSR energy-saving training has two parts: energy management and energy-saving technologies. The first focuses on the issue of how to build an energy management system, which departments should be involved and what the responsibilities are for each department. The second focuses on relevant energy-saving technologies and manufacturing process transformations. The trainers also arrange visits to demonstration companies that have implemented advanced energy technologies.

The evolution of the EEP project matches the development of the sustainability movement in China. The initial purpose was to help companies increase their energy efficiency awareness and the ability to manage their energy consumption. Traditionally, the purpose of energy management was to ensure sufficient energy supplies for production and product quality. Many including business, government and consumers thought that the call to reduce energy was simply driven by the desire to reduce carbon emissions – clearly underestimating the complexity of carbon footprints. The concept of reducing energy consumption during the manufacturing process has only recently emerged as central to process innovation as well. BSR now offers on-site energy assessments because many manufacturers lack the technical capability to identify energy-saving opportunities within their companies.

BSR considers EEP projects from the supply chain's perspective. They start with multinational corporations which may achieve energy savings and GHG emission reductions through their influence on suppliers. BSR does not yet have Chinese government involvement in this project.

WWF's Climate Savers programme, which HP joined in 2008, aims to reduce total carbon emissions in product supply chains. Karen Ho of WWF Hong Kong, a business engagement leader of the Climate Programme, sees the relationship between WWF and HP as "a facilitator or catalyst. We show best practices and hope for an ambitious attitude. HP's brand could influence the entire supply chain. If all HP's suppliers join in the carbon emission reduction activities the impact will become greater." To support companies with supply chain management, WWF has a special programme called Low Carbon Mission Production (LCMP) targeted at manufacturers.

As is widely known, carbon emissions during the manufacturing process can be very high. While the Climate Savers initiative champions the idea of carbon emission reduction, the LCMP looks at a factory as a unit and is specifically for multinational companies who are sourcing in China and aiming to manage their carbon emissions in their supply chains. WWF worked with HP to provide training to its suppliers, including sub-tiers. In order to do this, WWF and HP organized a workshop with 35 suppliers in 2011.

This two-day training included a number of issues, namely how to calculate carbon emissions, what the impact is on factories due to climate change, and what can be done to reduce carbon emissions. Focusing on best practices, all the suppliers participating made their own action plan by the end of the event.

WWF provides training in four areas:

1. Raising questions related to climate change: what is climate change? Is it an opportunity or an uncertainty for the manufacturing industry? Participants are required to discuss and perform reasoned analysis.

2. Learning about corporate carbon footprints from two different perspectives:

   a. From the factory's point of view, what are their carbon emission levels? How can greenhouse gas inventory be better controlled, where are the major sources of carbon emission generated and how may the total carbon footprint of the factory be calculated? Based on UN Global Compact protocol, the participants divide carbon emission sources in the factories into Scope 1, 2 and 3.

   b. Next, the carbon footprint is analysed from the product's perspective, addressing the issue of how to reduce carbon emissions during manufacturing. Teaching is based on real product examples with exercises on how to better analyse product carbon footprints. After training, suppliers have a clear understanding of how to calculate the carbon footprint within their factories.

3. Training on how to achieve a reduction in energy consumption or increased energy efficiency in factories. Through sharing business cases, participants identify

different systems in a factory to be analysed such as electricity, air conditioning or steam systems. Together with the trainers, the suppliers are required to analyse the factory's information from different angles and systems, and explore methods of reducing energy consumption and increase energy efficiency. As part of the training, suppliers are provided with effective plans such as installing "service notice advice" in their manufacturing devices.

4. Introduction to a number of strategies to identify which actions might be workable, require low investment, have a short return on investment (ROI) period, or are relatively easy to implement. The action plan should focus on what managers need to remember when bringing the plans back to their factories after the training.

HP also invited some outstanding suppliers to share their best practices on how to carry out an energy-saving programme. This is a valuable tool because it can set up a platform for suppliers to learn from each other. In addition, HP has an internal Enterprise Services team ready to provide energy and sustainability solutions to suppliers.

2.4.3 Working with Chinese governments

Through the EEP programme, HP suppliers are being taught energy management free of charge. There are also additional opportunities for HP's suppliers in China to mobilize resources, for example, through involving local government. In the words of Victor Cui, VP for Government Relationships at HP China, "The Chinese government pays much attention to environmental protection these days. There are several ministries responsible for this area, including the Ministry of Industry and Communication, the Ministry of

Environmental Protection and the Ministry of Science and Technology." The interaction is organized as follows:

- Macro-level policy at the central governmental level has a strong strategic drive focusing on companies including MNCs

- Chinese government agencies (corresponding ministries) are rolling out environmental standards

- These standards are represented in public procurement requirements

As a foreign company, HP complies with and supports all policy levels. HP also provides some advice on the mismatch between Chinese and international standards and suggests there could be a "grace period" for the Chinese industries to catch up with international standards.

HP helps suppliers interested in the EEP to compete for financial assistance and mobilize resources provided by the local or Hong Kong government authorities for driving energy efficiency programmes. While working on resource strategies, HP also assists suppliers in developing action plans on a regular basis, calculating how much energy the supplier can save during a certain time-frame. Such action plans often become the starting point for collecting initial data and for tracking the impact of energy management.

For those suppliers who want to join the EEP, HP suggests completing an energy audit to understand their starting point. It is important to know how much energy a particular site purchases, how it can minimize energy usage, how the savings should be used and subsequently translated into further investment.

2.4.4 Working with consultancies to analyse, improve and train suppliers

HP encourages its suppliers to work with energy consulting firms. As an example, HP invited CLP[4] Energy Services to conduct an energy audit and deliver training at a supplier event which over 180 participants attended and learned to use energy-saving tools such as ESCOs.[5] Through this experience, HP learned about the processes needed to achieve energy efficiency and sustainable energy consumption. HP summarized its own and its suppliers' best energy-saving practices and has since successfully transferred that knowledge to its supply chain. After the trial programme using consultants, HP decided to expand the programme throughout additional supplier tiers and achieve expanded progress going forward.

At the beginning of the EEP project, the focus was on energy consumption data from 50 factories among HP's Tier 1 suppliers. Before any training, HP completes a questionnaire survey to assess suppliers' existing calculation systems. Namely, what kind of calculation system, software and hardware is available, and how, for instance, the suppliers analyse their ROI when investing US$1 million or more.

HP's experience shows that Tier 1 suppliers invest considerable resources in data management. Normally, these Tier 1 suppliers achieve more savings than those sub-tiers because they have better awareness and are more willing to invest in energy saving. Most of the Tier 1 suppliers calculate their energy costs and some electronics factories are extremely cautious about cost control.

---

4   CLP is a leading responsible energy provider in the Asia–Pacific region: see https://www.clpgroup.com.

5   Energy service companies (ESCOs) are a practical way to obtain and finance energy-saving projects; the ESCOs guarantee that a certain amount of savings will be generated from the increased efficiency of the new equipment or via implementing energy improvement projects.

Consultancies help HP to examine the current status of the suppliers' factories, what factories can do in the future and where other resources could be saved. They can also help HP locate data for future projects. Brian Ou commented:

> The suppliers have no idea about macro information. What we do is that we tell them what opportunities they might have, through which way or channels they may find those opportunities and methods, how to identify if those methods are workable, what economic benefits they can get and what the return on investment will be.

Currently factories seem more willing to invest in the measurement of energy usage by real time monitoring systems, the cost of which is two or three times higher than normal monitoring systems. The main issue for many factories is how to turn such big investments into real process improvements. The reality is that many suppliers manufacture just one brand of product, in one building. Thus they have to bear the cost of a monitoring system on this narrow base. Once data has been collected and the costs have been calculated, the problem is not only how to make good use of this data but how to demonstrate that it will benefit energy management and control.

2.4.5 Applying an environmental management tool

For those suppliers that participated in the EEP and have already started their environmental work or showed an interest, HP is attempting to support more sustainable management with the help of the Global Social Compliance Programme (GSCP).[6] GSCP is a multi-industry global organization of different companies coming

---

6   See http://www.gscpnet.com/about-the-gscp/about-the-gscp.html.

together to develop guidance tools and best practice information on social and also on environmental issues.

By using GSCP's environmental reference tools, HP focuses on:

- Supplier environmental management systems

- Energy use and transport

- Water use

- Waste-water

- Emissions to air

- Waste management

- Incident prevention

- Management of contaminated land

- Biodiversity

GSCP defines three levels of supplier sustainability performance and provides suppliers with the tools and guidance to reach each level. Suppliers complete self-assessment questionnaires to determine what level of performance they currently exhibit. Suppliers that achieve Level 1 performance are aware of expectations and comply with legal requirements in each of the environmental impact categories. Level 2 is proactive management and performance improvement. Level 3 is leading practice. At the Level 3 performance level, suppliers go above and beyond standard practice. As highlighted by Sofia Kelly, HP Supply Chain Environmental Sustainability Programme Manager:

> HP wants their suppliers to achieve a Level 2 performance, thereby showing proactive environmental management. We want them to reach Level 3 in the energy provision of the GSCP because this is an area where HP and our suppliers have been focusing attention for several years.

HP first requests a completed GSCP self-assessment question-naire, and then allows the supplier to implement improvement programmes to reach the required performance levels. Once this is complete, the supplier may choose to be reviewed by a GSCP panel of experts. This panel reviews the supplier's information for accuracy and validity which confirms if the supplier has met the required level. HP implemented the GSCP programme in 2012 together with the 12 supplier locations that also participated in the first round of the EEP.

Sofia Kelly continues, "We're seeing companies' awareness of energy efficiency growing, and it's generally widespread in many countries including China. Suppliers are now beginning to focus efforts on other areas of environmental concern, such as water use, pollution, and waste."

2.5 Case studies showing collaboration between HP China and two of its suppliers

2.5.1 Jabil

Jabil is a global provider of electronics manufacturing services, with headquarters in St Petersburg, Florida. It has 60 factories around the world, with 165,000 employees and US$15.8 billion revenue in the 2014 fiscal year. HP has been a customer since 1998. Jabil provides finished products in two business areas: printed circuit board assembly (PCBA) and printers. Jabil presents an innovative and scientific approach to energy management.

During a visit to Jabil Huangpu in China, we were accompanied by Mr Xinchao Zhou, local facility manager at the factory and responsible for environment, health and security management. Mr Zhou said, "HP is an important customer for us and they ask for our energy-saving analysis report every month especially focusing on HP energy usage".

HP has installed different levels of control over production, although the facilities and workers belong to Jabil. HP closely monitors production, and leads work-space design and energy efficiency projects. The data collected at one factory site can be compared not only with other factories producing similar products but with the same supplier or other suppliers during previous periods. Comparing suppliers' performance helps to single out best practices; if one supplier does better than another then they can learn from the best performer. Co-location of production lines allows this comparison to take place, as it does in Jabil Huangpu.

The Huangpu factory in Guangzhou, currently one of Jabil's largest manufacturing sites, employs some 13,000 employees. The site's electricity consumption had increased by 1.3% in 2012, at the time of our visit, compared with 2011. Water usage had decreased by 5.2%, water vapour decreased by 20.9%, the use of natural gas decreased by 11.2%, and the use of nitrogen had reduced by 5.4% in that one year. While Jabil's total number of workers had increased by 7.5% and production volumes were up 9.3%, the absolute energy consumption of the factory decreased with a total saving of US$480,000 in that year alone.

In 2008, Jabil installed an energy sub-metering system on its HP production lines. Other customers soon followed. Before the new system was installed, the energy-cost calculation was based on the working space or cells that each client owned. By installing the meters, HP significantly reduced its nitrogen bill, as the system can control the actual consumption level. Jabil now calculates the energy consumption separately for each customer and the cost structure is transparent to all clients, including HP. The energy used is calculated as kilowatts per square foot, and the energy used by each customer is calculated based on renting the energy consumption per square foot. According to Xinchao Zhou, "Our customers have been pushing us to reduce prices annually, so our culture of continuously improving efficiency must go on due to the pressure from customers, competitors and society."

Jabil also installed energy meters in each dormitory room where employees live. This does not affect the costs to individual workers, but it gives them an idea of the energy consumed. Jabil ranks the consumption in each room. If some of the rooms are highly ranked, the employees will need to do a self-assessment and the human resources department will get involved to educate workers about a greener way of life. In this way, employees' energy-saving awareness is increased. Last year, Jabil paid for employee education and provided a manual on how energy is consumed at the factory. "We got high returns on a small investment. The average electricity consumption per capita reduced from 76 kWh in 2009 to 53 kWh in 2012," said Zhou.

By Chinese standards, the quality of employee accommodation at Jabil Huangpu is high, and working and living conditions in the electronics industry in general are far better than in other industries. Jabil, for example, provides workers with hot water available for showering 24 hours a day. In 2010 the company installed what it calls a "vapour system", a waste heat recovery system, in each building. Cost savings allowed the company to increase employee salaries. The next year Jabil introduced another heat recovery system, using hot air produced during manufacturing to heat water for dormitories. This, combined with a new solar-powered hot water system, reduced vapour usage, cut gas consumption by 9.1% and further raised awareness of green issues.

For Chinese suppliers this was a big step forward, Zhou explained:

> First, we calculated how much electricity, gas and water had been used to generate the hot water. Second, we encouraged our employees to save energy. Our standard hot water usage for

each employee is 50L per headcount each day. If 100L of hot
water is used, our energy consumption will increase. So, water
is closely linked to energy. If less water is used, less energy
would be used.

To illustrate, Xinchao Zhou outlined the energy usage distribution
in 2010 in regard to five major energy resources. Electricity accounted
for 55.6%, steam vapour for 22.6%, nitrogen for 16.7%, natural
gas for 4.6% and water for 0.5%. From electricity consumption, air
conditioning accounted for 45%, manufacturing for 25%, lighting for
18%, accommodation for 8% and compressed air for 3–5%. Steam
vapour is mainly used in air conditioning systems and accommodation. Air conditioning accounted for 80%, unsurprising considering the location of the Huangpu factory in humid South China,
and accommodation accounted for 4%. Nitrogen is mainly used in
a reflow oven. Natural gas was equally shared between the kitchens
and the accommodation. As for water, dormitories accounted for
52%, air conditioning accounted for 31%, kitchen accounted for 5%,
offices accounted for 1% and other greenery accounted for 11%.

Jabil ranks and scores the factors contributing to energy efficiency
by group: staff, equipment, management and process. "Management and processes turn out to be the most important point, even if
we have the best equipment and technology. Without management,
efficiency would be very low. The awareness of staff is also important," says Zhou. Jabil is currently improving a number of energy
controls and a management programme focused on measurement,
staff training, management team optimization, facilities, human
resources and work cells. Figure 2.1 shows the organizational structure of Jabil's energy management team.

Jabil also installed an automatic metering system and 209 digital
electric meters to increase the efficiency of meter reading and
analysis, which could optimize device operation. Among other
measures, the metering system suggested:

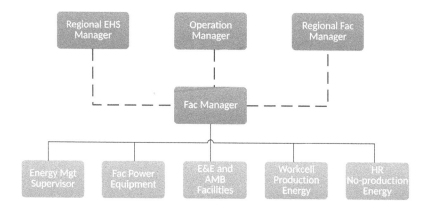

FIGURE 2.1 Jabil's energy management team

Source: Jabil; used with permission.

- Replacement of an old compressor and upgrade of two others

- Monthly checks for leakage and repair, decreasing the leakage rate from 0.8% to 0.5% resulting in CO_2 reduction up to 22 metric tonnes and achieving an annual cost saving of US$20,000

- Solar panel installation covering 1,200 m² in dormitories, providing 1,740 m³ of hot water per month and 20,900 m³ annually, thus reducing CO_2 emissions by 691 tonnes and achieving an annual cost saving of US$40,000

- Recycling wasted heat from the compressor thus reducing CO_2 by up to 450 metric tonnes and achieving a cost savings of US$40,000 every six months

Jabil's success lies in the fact that it has a system of implementing its energy efficiency programme (Fig. 2.2), composed of:

- Monitoring and measuring energy consumption

Item	Contents	Y	Schedule																				
			2011												2012							
		M	Jan	Feb	Mar	Apr	May	Jun	Jul	Aug	Sep	Oct	Nov	Dec	Jan	Feb	Mar	Apr	May	Jun	Jul
Define	Define goal	Plan																				
Measure		Do																				
Analysis	Collect history energy data	Plan																				
		Do																				
	Analyze issues	Plan																				
		Do																				
Improve	Install electricity meters and monitor system	Plan																				
		Do																				
	Auto monitor system trial run	Plan																				
		Do																				
	Set up WI for the system	Plan																				
		Do																				
	Install solar energy hot water for 7# dorm	Plan																				
		Do																				
	Replace electricity humidiffer by stream humidiffer	Plan																				
		Do																				
	Recycle waste heat from compressor for hot water supply in #8 dorm	Plan																				
		Do																				
Control	Weekly/Monthly Energy Analysis	Plan																				
		Do																				
	User take action for energy control	Plan																				
		Do																				
	Set up energy monitor center in other site	Plan																				
		Do																				

FIGURE 2.2   Annual energy-saving plan at Jabil

Source: Jabil; used with permission.

- A supportive organizational structure

- Analysis of the data collected

- Reporting to energy users

Additionally, Jabil has a Supplier Quality Team helping thousands of suppliers to improve their practices by achieving ISO 14000 and ISO 18000 standards. To comply with environmental targets, Jabil signs EHS (Environment, Health and Safety) agreements with sub-suppliers. These include waste and chemical materials disposal.

Zhou sums up as follows:

> Actually, I think the intelligent monitoring system is only a tool. The most important thing is management. We use the closed-loop principle and apply the quality assurance theory which is plan, do, check, act and then return again, improving our energy performance. When you find a signal of deviation, you modify it.

For example, Jabil found that the use of steam did not save as much energy as they had expected. There turned out to be a small device failure meaning that the hot water did not go where intended. Solar panels prevented the pump from working so the water could not pass through, which caused two weeks of wasted energy.

> Measuring is also important, and we have to let the staff understand our concepts. Now the staff will take the initiative to analyse such situations. Because they know that their management cares about this. Once employees have ideas, we provide money and give our permission to support them. Employees will be passionate about carrying on with this.

2.5.2 Supplier A[7]

HP periodically visits its suppliers to check the progress of developing programmes. In this section, we describe a visit to one of its Tier 1 suppliers in East China, "Supplier A". Supplier A's products include motherboards, graphics cards and PCs. Their management representative commented on their relationship with HP:

> We benefit from working with and sharing best practice with world-class customers like HP. I often talk to my colleagues saying that we should be ahead of others in terms of CSR because our customers are all world leaders.

Supplier A now follows HP and other large corporations' manufacturing strategies and has moved its production towards western China, specifically to the city of Chongqing, where it can create new job opportunities. It participated in the EEP, and produced an action plan for energy reduction, spurred on by a local government requirement to reduce carbon emissions by 5% by 2013.

As an illustration of the importance of industry alliances, Supplier A emphasizes membership in the EICC: "As a member, we follow EICC protocols and collaborate with HP on many EICC

7   The real name of "Supplier A" has been disguised at the request of the company.

initiatives, for example, energy and carbon reporting and the 'HER project' which helps suppliers care for the health of female workers." Supplier A also adopted environmental practices from the EICC. Before sourcing components from its Tier 2 suppliers, it normally requires suppliers to sign a code of conduct requiring them to follow EICC and their requirements, Chinese law and regulations in all aspects of CSR. Supplier A will always monitor suppliers' performance to control legal requirements and environmental regulations.

Supplier A worked with HP to promote EEP for Tier 2 suppliers in 2012, bringing in a total of 23 suppliers and 47 participants. All participating Tier 2 suppliers have now provided their action plans on energy savings. The manager in charge at the Supplier A site explained, "When we select suppliers, CSR is one rating category. CSR includes labour rights, health and safety, and environmental capacity building. We do an environmental audit every two years on all our suppliers." Supplier A also checks whether suppliers have international environmental certification such as ISO 14001 or other environment-related certifications.

2.6 The final word

The situation in the electronics industry is austere as very few electronics OEMs look beyond the first tier for environmental code of conduct implementation. Indeed, due to the complicated nature of electronics supply chains, it is difficult for any OEM to fully implement an energy efficiency programme throughout the entire supply chain. However, through stakeholder engagement and knowledge transfer with the help of non-governmental organizations, environmental consultancies, industrial standard organizations and partnering with suppliers, HP has proved that significant improvements can be made.

2.7 Case summary

Hewlett-Packard has developed an innovative "green supply chain" in China which has benefited not only the company itself but the many companies that are part of its supply chain in China. HP is thus a classic example of how practices developed in one company can be rolled out across an entire supply chain or value chain to affect many other companies and communities as well. Key to success here has been HP's willingness to collaborate and work with its local partners in China. Important features of the green supply chain include:

- Use of advanced technology and services to help customers reduce CO_2 emissions

- Leveraging its position as the world's largest provider of IT infrastructure, software and services to help companies turn energy consumption data into usable information

- Public disclosure of its own supply chain carbon footprint, the first company in the electronics industry to do so

- Developing an industry-wide carbon and energy data collection system that collect information from 81% of its suppliers by spend

- Reduction of suppliers' greenhouse gas emissions through energy efficiency training and development

3
Sourcing strategy in China: Nestlé

3.1 Introduction

Nestlé is a consumer-oriented food and nutrition company with headquarters in Vevey, Switzerland. It is the largest food company in the world by revenue. Nestlé was founded in 1905 by the merger of Anglo-Swiss Milk Company, established in 1866, and Farine Lactée Henri Nestlé, founded in 1867. The company grew significantly during the first half of the last century, eventually expanding its offerings beyond its early condensed milk and infant formula products to include coffee, tea, bottled water, breakfast cereals, confectionery, dairy products, ice cream, pet foods and snacks. Today, Nestlé operates about 450 factories in 86 countries, and employs around 328,000 people. Its revenue in 2014 was US$93.6 billion.

Nestlé has a number of subsidiaries including Crosse & Blackwell, Findus, Libby's, Rowntree Mackintosh and Gerber. It has a primary listing on the SIX Swiss Exchange, is a constituent of the Swiss Market Index and has a secondary listing on Euronext. Nestlé is consistently ranked in the top 100 of the Fortune 500 list of most

1988	Building of Nestlé Dong Guan plant.
1989	Nestlé signed an agreement with Pu'er government valid for 14 years providing training on coffee production.
1992	The Agricultural Service Team was set up, expatriate manager John Patter appointed and based in Kunming.
1997	1. The buying station was set up in Pu'er. 2. The Demonstration and Experimental Farm in Jing Hong was set up. 3. All the Arabica coffee bean supply was from Yunnan.
2002	The agricultural service and buying station was relocated from Kuming to Pu'er.
2005	Wouter De Smet took over from his father Jan De Smet becoming the fifth Agricultural Service Team manager.
2012	Nestlé purchased a record of 100,500 tonnes of coffee beans at the 2011/12 buying season from Yunnan (mainly Pu'er).

TABLE 3.1   Milestones for Nestlé's coffee procurement in Yunnan

valuable companies in the world by gross revenue. The company seeks to be recognized as the world leader in Nutrition, Health and Wellness, trusted by all its stakeholders, and to be the industry reference for financial performance. This is not just about size: the company aims to be known and trusted for exemplary behaviour, encapsulated in the simple phrase, "Good Food, Good Life".

Nestlé works to achieve market leadership and earn trust by satisfying customer and stakeholder expectations as well as creating shared value for its business partners and the communities in which it operates. Over the years, consumers have evolved from simply wanting "good food" (meaning safe, wholesome, convenient and affordable) to seeking a more sophisticated set of attributes, including a sense of wellbeing, physical wellness and psychological comfort. Nestlé has aimed to strengthen consumers' trust in the company and its products, increasing brand loyalty. In recent years, this has expanded to include environmental and social sustainability, along with its own financial stability. Nestlé seeks to bring these sensibilities to its coffee operations in China.

The company mainly uses local materials to produce foods of the same quality as imported products, eliminating foreign exchange tariffs. Ninety-nine per cent of Nestlé products in China are produced in China. Today, Nestlé has 33 Chinese factories, two of them processing coffee (one in Dong Guan, the other in Qing Dao; see Table 3.1).

3.2 China's coffee-growing regions

Coffee was introduced to Yunnan Province in south-west China in 1902 by a French missionary. Over the course of nearly a century, successful cultivation led to plantations, and as more farmers planted the crop, an industry developed. Yunnan province still accounts for 98% of China's coffee production, with the other 2% grown in Hainan, the country's southernmost province. Because of its limited planting area and environmental conditions, coffee production from Hainan is of lower quality and quantity than that of Yunnan.

Yunnan borders Vietnam, Burma and Laos and is populated by many ethnic minorities. Due to its unique environment and geology, Pu'er (a prefecture in Yunnan) provides the best place to grow coffee in the province. In Pu'er, farmers have lived in relative poverty and until recently most earned a living on tea plantations. Nearly 100% of Yunnan's coffee bean production is Arabica, predominately of the Catimor hybrid, which prospers in slightly acid soil with a pH value of 4.5–5.5, as found throughout Pu'er. In addition, coffee requires sufficient moisture and a frost-free season to foster good growth. The region is unsuitable for most other varieties because of the risk of coffee leaf rust and the high altitude and mountainous terrain, which experiences frequent frost during the winter.

Year	Planting area (hectares)	Production (tons)
2003	20,062	20,207
2004	20,000	21,000
2007	23,333	28,500
2008	25,333	30,000
2009	26,667	40,000

TABLE 3.2 Coffee planting areas and coffee tonnage in Yunnan Province, 2003–2009

Source: The International Trade Centre (2010). *The Coffee Sector in China: An Overview of Production, Trade and Consumption.*

In 2012 the total coffee planting area in Yunnan province was around 68,000 hectares (1,020,000 mu).[1] Coffee output was about 36,500 tonnes and the value of Yunnan's coffee industry totalled RMB 900 million. In 2010, 54% of the coffee area (mainly around Baoshan) was hit by a severe drought. According to the *Yunnan Daily News*, 40% of the new coffee saplings planted in 2009 withered and died as a result. The total economic loss was estimated at about US$88 million, and the drought continued to impact the quality and quantity of output in 2011 and 2012. But although production was down in Baoshan, it was unaffected in Pu'er. In fact, the total production of Yunnan increased as a result of new plantings (see Table 3.2).

3.3 Nestlé in China

Nestlé opened its first sales office in Shanghai in 1980, the first Western brand to enter the country as it undertook massive economic

---

1   Chinese unit of area roughly equating to 0.16 of an acre or 647 m².

changes. Around the same time, the company began to consult the government about investing in China, including building factories and sharing technology and information about nutrition and food processing. In 1988, the Dong Guan joint venture plant was built in Dong Guan, Guangdong province. After that Nestlé started to build factories across the country supplying products from nutritional items to water, and ice cream to confectionery.

In 1988, after extensive research and investigation, Nestlé identified parts of Yunnan province as ideal places to grow coffee and decided to support the development of coffee production. In 1989 Nestlé Dong Guan signed an agreement with the Pu'er government to provide coffee production training. In 1992, Nestlé created an Agricultural Service Team in Kunming (the capital of Yunnan) and started with a coffee development programme that focused on training and technical assistance. In 1997 the company set up a small coffee-buying station and dry mill in Pu'er and a demonstration and experimental farm in Jing Hong, Xi Shuang Ban Na prefecture in Yunnan. Five years later, the agricultural service centre was relocated and consolidated with the buying station in Pu'er. In the 2011–12 buying season, after a decade of growth, Nestlé bought a record 10,500 tonnes of green coffee in China, mainly from Pu'er.

3.3.1 The coffee market in China

In 2009, the retail sales volume of coffee in China was slightly more than 30,000 tonnes – just over 0.02 kg per capita – totalling US$694 million. A growing urban population (600 million people) accounts for an estimated 90% of the country's coffee consumption, raising annual per capita consumption by the target market to around 0.05 kg.

Although there has been a consistent increase in consumption of roasted and ground coffee in recent years, instant coffee (including

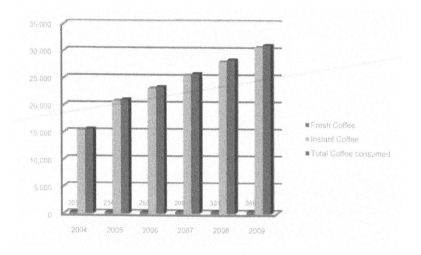

FIGURE 3.1   Retail sales of coffee by type, 2004–2009

Source: The International Trade Centre (2010). *The Coffee Sector in China: An Overview of Production, Trade and Consumption.*

"3-in-1": that is, coffee, sugar and creamer) still accounts for well over 90% of consumption, with some estimates as high as 99% (see Figure 3.1). Fresh coffee remains a niche category thanks to the immature coffee culture, high prices and the low penetration of coffee machines. Fresh coffee is primarily consumed in cafés and restaurants because most Chinese coffee drinkers do not know how to brew coffee or do not want to invest in a coffee machine. In addition, Chinese coffee drinkers tend to eat while they drink, so "coffee-to-go" sales are not as prevalent as in Western countries (though they are on the rise).

In 2009, Nestlé launched single-cup packaging for instant coffee and made it widely available in convenience stores in China's more developed cities. While coffee consumption in China has been somewhat dependent on its café culture (see Box 3.1), sales of fresh coffee, which includes fresh-ground as well as whole beans, rose by

Box 3.1: China's café culture

- Coffee house regulars are mostly young (20–40 years), affluent, fashion-conscious, urban Chinese. Foreign travellers and expatriates account for 15–25% of coffee house customers.

- Chinese patrons of gourmet and speciality coffee houses prefer lattes, cappuccinos and mochas to espressos, which they consider to be too bitter.

- Coffee-themed casual dining restaurants, such as DIO Coffee and New Island Coffee, experienced booming popularity in the early 2000s, and are still very common in most first and second-tier cities in China. This is not necessarily because of an increase in coffee consumption, and is possibly due to the popularity of coffee-house-style atmosphere.

- Chinese primarily go to coffee shops for:
  - Music and ambience
  - Branded wares – coffee mugs, thermoses, etc.
  - Variety of fresh pastries, cookies, etc.

- Most Chinese patrons in coffee shops are:
  - Business people meeting
  - Friends meeting
  - Couples (on a date)

an average of 12% per year from 2004 to 2009. And while the rate of increase declined by 1–2% each year during that period, the low base sales of fresh coffee make it difficult to forecast whether this trend will continue.

Nestlé has established a 68% share of the instant coffee market in China. Recently, other companies such as Kraft Foods and Maxwell House have started to buy more Yunnan Arabica beans from local trade. Nestlé and Guangzhou Kraft accounted for more than 80% of retail coffee sales in China in 2009 (see Table 3.3). This trend has been consistent for several years. Nestlé's dominant market share is largely attributed to its early arrival in the market, the fact that

Company	Coffee brands	2009
Nestlé (China) Ltd	Nescafé	68
Guangzhou Kraft Food Co., Ltd	Maxwell House	14
Jiangsu Mocca Food Co., Ltd	Mocca	1
Dalian UCC Ueshima Coffee Co., Ltd	UCC	1
Shantou Gold Roast Food International Co., Ltd	Bencafé	<1
Hainan Haikou Lisheng Coffee & Foods Co., Ltd	Lisun	<1
Changzhou Super Coffee Beverage Co., Ltd	Super	<1
Others	-	14
Total		**100**

TABLE 3.3   Estimated coffee company shares 2009, percentage of retail value

Source: The International Trade Centre (2010). *The Coffee Sector in China: An Overview of Production, Trade and Consumption.*

it set up a Nescafé factory in Dong Guan and its very successful marketing and sales activities in the country. To some extent, it is difficult for domestic players to compete with the larger multinational companies (see Table 3.4).

3.3.2 Agricultural reform in China

In 1992, local governments began to liberalize both procurement and retail prices in agricultural markets, which finally ended the unified procurement and marketing system for grain and other agricultural products across the country. Since 2004, the government has formulated several agriculture policies to facilitate development and improve the living standard for farmers. "San Nong",[2]

---

2   San Nong (三农 in Chinese): three dimensions of rural issues, including agriculture, rural development and peasants, first proposed by Dr Tiejun Wen in 1996 and later widely adopted by the government. It impacts on such issues as the inequality between cities and rural areas, welfare of peasant worker immigrants and agricultural infrastructure development in China.

Company	Area	Ownership type	Turnover (US$ m)	Brands	Coffee-related business	Product scope
Nestlé Guangdong Co., Ltd	Guangdong	Foreign investment	343.21	Nescafé, Nespresso	Processor, coffee retail shops	Instant coffee powder, 3-in-1 coffee powder
Kraft Guangdong Food Co., Ltd	Guangdong	Foreign investment	22.37	Maxwell House	Processor	Instant coffee powder, 3-in-1 coffee powder
Changzhou Super Coffee	Jiangsu	Foreign investment	13.36	Super	Processor	Instant oatmeal, instant coffee, compound beverage, expanded food, milk, tea
Zhuhai Jierong Food Co., Ltd	Guangdong	Joint venture	9.67	TWG	Processor	Coffee beans, coffee powder, English-style tea powder, coffee machines
Mocca Food Co., Ltd	Jiangsu	Foreign investment	8.85	Mocca	Processor	Coffee production
Hainan Haikou Lisheng Coffee & Foods Co., Ltd	Hainan	Shareholding	3.58	Lisun	Processor	Instant coffee powder, 3-in-1 coffee powder, coconut powder
Yunnan Coffee Co., Ltd	Yunnan	State owned	1.92	Leshou, Jin Xiagu	Processor	Roasted coffee beans, R&G coffee powder
Beijing G.E.O. Coffee Co., Ltd	Beijing	Foreign investment	1.77	GEO	Processor	Roasted coffee beans, instant coffee powder
Shanghai Dehui Food Co., Ltd	Shanghai	Foreign investment	1.35	Yuanshuai	Processor	Roasted coffee beans, instant coffee powder, 3-in-1 coffee powder, sugar
Ruixu Food (Shanghai) Co., Ltd	Shanghai	Foreign investment	1.31	Ruichang	Processor	Instant coffee powder, coffee mate, other soft drinks

TABLE 3.4   Coffee companies, brands and turnover

Source: The International Trade Centre (2010). *The Coffee Sector in China: An Overview of Production, Trade and Consumption.*

the coordinated development of farms and villages along with general agriculture, is the umbrella term for these policies. It considers agricultural production, the condition of rural areas and the population from several angles, such as the status of the farms, farmers' quality of life, the local economy and environmental impacts and changes.

In 2006, the Law of the People's Republic of China on Farmer's Specialized Co-operatives was enacted to reflect and formalize the San Nong policy. This law took effect in 2007. The objectives of the law include regulating the behaviours of Farmer's Specialized Co-operatives, protecting the lawful rights of the Farmer's Specialized Co-operatives and their members and improving agricultural and rural development. The law defines a Farmer's Specialized Co-operative as a mutual assistance economic organization formed on the principle of voluntary and democratic management by the producers, service providers and users of an agricultural product. It stipulates building on rural household lease operations, and instructs central and local governments to subsidize the co-ops by providing training, certification of agricultural products, investment in agricultural infrastructure and sales and marketing of agricultural products. Priority is given to underdeveloped rural areas, minority ethnic group areas, and remote and border areas. The law also focuses on the most needed agricultural products. The law defines the legal status of co-ops and empowers them to trade and conduct business.

In 2012, under the 12th Five-Year Plan, the Chinese government began to invest heavily in agricultural production and rural development. These measures included increasing agriculture subsidies, waiving taxes on production and supporting the development of agricultural technology.

3.4 Nestlé's coffee sourcing process in Pu'er

3.4.1 Coffee processing

An understanding of the coffee production process is key to appreciating the issues involved in sourcing and supply. Coffee beans from different varieties and regions have their own distinct aroma, body, acidity and nuances of flavour. These characteristics depend not only on geography and environment, but also on how they are processed. The fruit of the coffee tree is called a cherry. Each cherry usually contains two beans, covered by:

1. A silver skin

2. A layer of parchment

3. A mucilaginous flesh (pulp and mucilage)

4. The outer skin, red or yellow when the fruit is ripe (see Figure 3.2)

The first step of coffee processing is cherry-picking. In Yunnan picking is normally done by hand, which costs around RMB 2 per

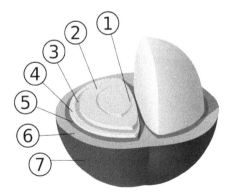

Structure of coffee berry:
1. Centre cut
2. Bean (endosperm)
3. Silver skin (testa, epidermis)
4. Parchment (hull, endocarp)
5. Pectin layer
6. Pulp (mesocarp)
7. Outer skin (pericarp, exocarp)

FIGURE 3.2   Structure of coffee cherry

Source: Y. Tambe, licensed under BY-SA 2.0.

kilo. Layers 3 and 4 must be removed by one of two methods, dry or wet processing. For Arabica, the most common variety in Pu'er, the wet processing method is most commonly employed. The outer layer and the pulp are torn off by squeezing the cherries through a pulper, but the beans will still have a significant amount of mucilage clinging to them that must be removed at this stage. This is done either by the classic natural ferment-and-wash method or mechanically, which is a newer procedure and requires less water. After the pulp and mucilage have been removed, the parchment coffee must be dried to a moisture content of about 11% so as to preserve the beans safely in storage. Coffee beans can be dried mechanically or through sun drying. Once dry, the beans go through a dry milling process, which involves removing the last layers of parchment, silver skin and remaining residue from the dry coffee in a huller. The result is green coffee beans (the state of beans before they are roasted).

The majority of the coffee growers in Pu'er, including the small-scale farmers, do the whole process as described above at their own farms. Some small growers do the initial preparation themselves, and then sell the unprocessed coffee to intermediaries or big growers for the final step of dry milling. With the increase in coffee acreage, production volume and the introduction of responsible farming, more and more large growers are introducing eco-processing equipment that combines a pulper and a mechanical mucilage remover in order to improve efficiency and save water.

3.4.2 Coffee buying

The period from November to April is peak coffee-buying season in Yunnan. The Agricultural Service Team represents Nestlé in purchasing a certain amount of coffee there every year. The purchasing station is located in a national grain reserve in Pu'er, which is maintained by the local government. Nestlé was allocated a small office building and several warehouses within the reserve. Nestlé's trading price changes with fluctuations in the New York commodity exchange. Typically, Nestlé pays slightly less than the New York price and the company announces its coffee price every Monday and Thursday by sending text messages to all participating farmers. The price is determined independently and the process is transparent to all suppliers.

When the price rises, farmers queue up at the purchasing station with tricycles, (hand) tractors and trucks filled with coffee beans. The line can stretch almost 1½ km along the single-lane road between the main highway and the grain reserve. The beans are given batch numbers, one supplier at a time.

In buying from different suppliers, quality control is a critical step. All deliveries undergo multiple quality control tests before they are bought and processed for use in consumer products. The process mainly involves moisture assessment, defect analysis and cupping (roasting, grinding and tasting). Each bag offered by suppliers is sampled and undergoes a first visual quality assessment. If a bag is of significantly lower quality than the batch it will be rejected and if several such bags are found it will lead to rejection of the whole batch.

A sample of the delivery with its batch number will be sent to the laboratory where the first test is for moisture content. Coffee is divided into two grades, Q1 (from 9.5% to 12% moisture) and Q2 (12% to 12.5%). Beans with moisture levels above or below these limits are not accepted; beans that are too dry are fragile and do not roast well (and are more subject to defects), and beans that are too moist are vulnerable to fungus and bacteria. Q1 beans are slightly more expensive than Q2. After the moisture content is established, the number of defective (e.g. black, crushed, elephant, diseased and mouldy beans) is assessed.

The final component of quality control is cupping, in which at least four cupping experts from the Agricultural Service Team taste the coffee, evaluate the flavour and aroma and reach agreement on the taste. Then they decide whether to accept or reject the batch. The whole quality assessment is "blind" as none of the team in the laboratory knows the identity of the supplier. The result with the batch number is sent to the warehouse, where it will be linked to the supplier. A bonus/penalty scheme is applied to the farmers according to a fixed procedure to enhance continuous improvement of the quality.

If a batch passes all the tests, the beans will be re-bagged in standard Nestlé bags (70 kg), each printed with a batch number which includes supplier number, moisture level and defect level, enabling traceability. The supplier is paid for the total number of kilos plus the weight of the sample taken (1 kg per bag). Even after this, the beans are subject to two external rounds of testing by a Quality Testing Centre in Vietnam and the production plant's Quality Control Team.

The Nestlé purchasing process is transparent to the farmers and applies to all batches, big or small. This is not the case for many other companies who buy in Yunnan. Initially, there were very few companies performing the cupping test, and their judgements were subjective. Each company graded coffee by its own standard and paid a different price. Now, it is the consensus of the farmers that while it is difficult to become a Nestlé supplier and get into their system, once you get in the price paid is normally the highest and the payment term is excellent (cash on delivery for less than 10 tonnes and bank transfer within five working days for more than 10 tonnes). Nestlé quality and price have become a reference point for the Yunnan coffee trade.

3.5 Nestlé's coffee Agricultural Service Team

Nestlé's Agricultural Service Team was created in 1992, after the company had signed a 14-year agreement with the Pu'er government to train the local farmers to grow coffee and promising a certain procurement volume with a minimum price in 1989. There have been five team managers since then (John Pater, Hans Feassler, Maarten Warndorff, Jan De Smet and Wouter De Smet). John Pater searched for suitable plantation sites during his term and tested planting techniques; Feassler promoted coffee cultivation in Yunnan; Warndorff focused on training technical personnel; and Jan De Smet promoted purchasing from small-scale farmers and relocated the Agricultural Service Team from Kunming to Pu'er in order to be close to the supply in 2002. This was a crucial step in winning the trust of small farmers and creating the supply base as it now exists, on the grounds that, according to Nestlé Technical Assistance Executive Jiazhi Hou, "the Chinese only believe what can be seen". Nestlé relocated the Agricultural Service Team to Pu'er to convince the farmers of Nestlé's ongoing presence, thus increasing their confidence in the coffee market. Wouter De Smet, the current manager, says:

> you cannot ask a farmer who is producing three tons to bring his coffee to Kunming … The office was important for technical assistance … but the buying station was very important for the village communities because they had a reliable market.

The lineage and continuity of the agricultural team has also bred trust between Nestlé and its producers.

In 2012, there were eight people working full-time as members of the team: Wouter De Smet, a buying station executive, a warehouse operator, a logistics operator, a technical executive and a demonstration farm manager reporting to him. There was also an accountant and a secretary. In the coffee-buying season, three temporary

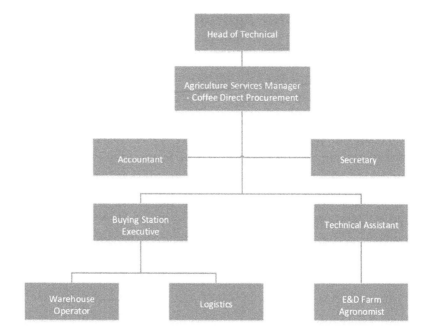

FIGURE 3.3   Nestlé Agricultural Service Team in Pu'er

members of staff are employed to work on quality control and at the warehouse to receive coffee beans (see Figure 3.3).

The Agricultural Service Team is supported technically by R&D centres in Tours, France and Singapore. The Nestlé Dong Guan plant receives technical support from R&D centres in Switzerland and the USA. Technical support includes recipe development, training and technical assistance for designing, building and equipping factories. The agricultural team is part of Dong Guan Plant administratively, but the head of the team is at the same hierarchical level as the GM in Dong Guan.

Since the start of the programme, agricultural technical assistance has cost US$6 million. In about the same time-span the total area planted with coffee grew tenfold in Yunnan province, and the quality improved considerably. Thanks to this achievement, the Dong Guan plant has been able to source all of its Arabica beans from Yunnan since 1997. Cooperation among governments, farmers and Nestlé was essential in achieving these goals. There are now more than 100,000 people in Yunnan involved in coffee agriculture, processing and trade. Since Yunnan is among the provinces with the lowest rural incomes, coffee has become an important source of income and has improved the standard of living. This is in line with the Nestlé creed that its activities can only benefit the company in the long term if they benefit that country or region where they do business. The company believes coffee represents tremendous potential for Yunnan, as coffee consumption in China is on the rise.

Opened in 1997, the Nestlé Experimental and Demonstration Farm is located near Jing Hong in Xi Shuang Ban Na prefecture, and is managed by the Agricultural Service Team. It covers 60 hectares, 20 of which are planted in coffee. The overall aim of the farm is to show farmers how to achieve higher yields of better quality in a responsible and sustainable way. Working with the Nestlé labs in France and Singapore, the farm carries out a number of activities:

- Testing new coffee varieties

- Carrying out trials on agricultural problems

- Experimenting with coffee stem borer control (the borer is an insect pest)

- Demonstrating a wide range of coffee cultivation and postharvest techniques (erosion control, environmental protection, pest and disease control, eco-processing and waste-water management)

- Providing theoretical and hands-on training to technicians and students of agriculture and food manufacture

- Giving guided tours to farmers' organizations, coffee companies and schools on request

- Providing coffee growers with seeds of superior coffee varieties

3.6 Nestlé's supply structure in Yunnan

The 1989 agreement Nestlé signed with the Pu'er government specified that Nestlé base its price for Yunnan coffee on the NY market price and set minimum prices to protect the growers. Nestlé also promised to provide technical support, coffee seeds and interest-free loans for agricultural equipment. In the early 1990s, there was a coffee company in each county of Pu'er. Nestlé could only buy coffee from these companies, part of a government-run system of Supply and Marketing Co-operatives (供销社) under the Chinese planned economy.

In 1992, when China began to abandon the planned economy and move towards the free market and privatization, the Supply and Marketing Co-operative system gradually faded away. Nestlé started to buy coffee directly from privatized coffee companies and individual farmers whose crops met their standards. The remaining state-owned coffee companies either sold the land to the farmers who were already working on it, or were privatized as a whole, becoming coffee-growing companies who also supplied Nestlé. These companies, whose land ranged from several hundred mu to 3,000 mu, often expanded their production and also bought coffee beans from individual farmers for export or sale to domestic buyers, including Nestlé.

The relocation of the agricultural team from Kunming to Pu'er in 2002 was a landmark event for Nestlé's procurement, making it much easier for farmers to sell their coffee beans. When the first farmers sold coffee to Nestlé and gained significant economic benefits, others followed, village by village. From then on, Nestlé's procurement ran on a small-farmer scale, marking an era of direct procurement from individual farmers. Now 99% of the suppliers are coffee growers; 80% are farmers with a farm under 50 mu or 3 ha. By 2012, the total number of suppliers had climbed to over 1,800, six times the number in 2005.

In 2006 the Nestlé agricultural team set up the supply traceability system: every qualified farmer is assigned a supplier code and given an identification card. The team keeps supplier records, with such information as supplier type, farm size, processing method, annual production, estimated production this year, fertilizer use and so on.

Dealing with small farmers not only encourages them to grow coffee, but also avoids intermediaries and channels profits directly to the farmers. However, the small-farmer model creates difficulties for Nestlé: some farmers have as few as eight coffee trees and sell the produce to Nestlé; while the cost of the coffee is predetermined, the cost of purchasing is high. In addition training so many small providers is not economical and quality is not standardized.

Encouraged by Nestlé, the "Farmer Group" has emerged as a new form of coffee production co-operative. Farmer groups are based on family farms or any coalition of small farmers who voluntarily take risks together and share any resulting benefits. A farmer group consists of three or more loosely organized households, typically including a dozen or so households whose coffee holdings are located in close proximity. In some cases, a whole village forms a farmer group (Farmer's Specialized Co-op), organized by the village committee and village branch of the China Communist Party (CCP) and constituted under the stipulation of co-op law; there is some overlap between these two forms of organization.

At a macro level, the government (including central, Yunnan provincial and Pu'er local governments) promotes the Farmer's Specialized Co-ops under the voluntary principle following the Farmer's Specialized Co-operatives law enacted in 2006. For example, in 2011, there were 62 co-ops registered with the Pu'er government. Fifty additional co-ops were formed during 2012.

As with the Supply and Marketing Co-operatives, Nestlé offers the less formal Farmer Groups a prenegotiated contract with guaranteed prices in order to avoid risks in purchasing and ensure the quality of their coffee supply. The formation of farmer groups helps regulate and standardize agricultural practices and quality; farmers invest collectively and promote their coffee brand (here, each farmer group considers their coffee a "brand", though clearly not a brand in the commercial sense). For example, requirements for a 1,000 mu farmer group include a minimum of 100 coffee sun drying racks spread out in a 5,000 m^2 yard and a waste-water treatment pool of at least 25 m^3. The government awards a bonus of RMB 10,000 for joining and RMB 50,000 for qualifying. This benefits Nestlé: it is easier to organize training through village committees, and coffee quality is more reliable. The farmer groups form the infrastructure, the Pu'er government provides financial and policy support and Nestlé provides training. (Here, the "farmer groups" also include Farmer's Specialized Co-ops.)

This system reverts to "traditional" policy in some ways, including tax structure and regulations similar to the Supply and Marketing Co-operatives. The Farmer's Specialized Co-operatives are supported by the government and operate like trading companies. The government offers a preferential policy to assist these co-operatives' development (see Figure 3.4). The difference between the government-promoted Farmer's Specialized Co-ops and the farmer groups supported by Nestlé is that the former is tighter and an economic organization in a real sense, while the latter is more

FIGURE 3.4   Nestlé's sourcing structure evolution in China

loosely structured. The latter could be viewed as a preliminary form of the former.

Purchasing coffee from farmer groups improves efficiency and reduces the workload for the Agricultural Service Team. It also reduces farmers' waiting time in the queue, especially during peak coffee season. On the other hand, Nestlé occasionally faces the risk of disruptions to its coffee supply due to some farmers reneging on prenegotiated contracts (i.e. future contracts), which state the quantity and price of the coffee beans to be bought by Nestlé during the buying season of the same year. For example, one farm group consisted of three siblings selling coffee to Nestlé according to the terms of their prenegotiated contract. However, as coffee prices rose on the spot market, one brother decided to sell to other companies for the higher price. His brothers were forced to fill the gap and borrow coffee beans from other farmers to avoid breaking the contract. While the other group members fulfilled the contract, such actions could expose Nestlé's supply chain to uncertainty by interrupting the coffee supply.

The coffee market in China continues to grow and change. Some other large companies buy beans in Yunnan, but most of them do not deal directly with farmers or Farmer Groups. Instead, they contract with established middlemen or local coffee companies to transact business. Overall, however, the market price is not significantly affected by the middlemen's pricing, and is transparent due to Nestlé's benchmark price and quality standards.

3.7 Creating shared value: rural development and water management

The Yunnan coffee project is considered an exemplar by Nestlé, and Yunnan is becoming the largest washed Arabica producer in Asia. The company aims to increase its work with the Pu'er government and the Pu'er coffee industry. Nestlé invested over RMB 50 million in the agricultural team and developing coffee plantations in Yunnan during 2012. In the early days, there were few roads in some areas and the team had to walk to many tiny villages, often staying overnight in farmers' homes. This is no longer the case, as infrastructure is vastly improved, due in large part to the growth of the coffee industry.

3.7.1 Supplier development

When Nestlé introduced the Agricultural Service Team in 1992, conditions were very difficult. Purchasing Executive Juecheng Luo says that "many locals didn't know what coffee was and had to be taught everything. Nestlé invited technicians from the coffee companies to a processing plant and provided them with training, free accommodation and meals." Later, more farmers grew coffee under the guidance of the coffee companies. The training was naturally extended to them. Nestlé takes different approaches to training different groups. Coffee company technicians get both theory and practice training. More concerned with results, farmers are less interested in theory so they learn only best practices.

Jiazhi Hou said "we teach the farmers everything we know regarding coffee growing and processing and risk-hedging ... And they can sell to anybody at any time – not just Nestlé." Over the years, company agronomists integrated their lives into Yunnan and its coffee plantations, helping farmers improve the quality of their products and their own lives. In fact, the current resident agronomist (Wouter De Smet) is called "Mr Coffee" or "Mr Nestlé" by local farmers. Nestlé also provides help with financial management and has advised farmers to diversify and avoid the risks and pitfalls of basing their businesses on a one-pillar economy. The company's development efforts extend to other areas, as well.

According to Juecheng Luo, local farmers now trust Nestlé. "Farmers trust us to the extent that once they deliver the coffee beans to our warehouse, they disappear. They don't worry about any opportunistic behaviour from us."

There are even feelings of gratitude and pride between the company, local coffee farmers and the government. Han Lu, Director of the Pu'er Coffee Office (a government agency) says:

> Nestlé has been paying great efforts in coffee plantation training, developing the coffee industry here and purchasing coffee in Pu'er. From an objective and historical point of view, without Nestlé, Pu'er coffee industry would not be as successful as it is today. We – the Pu'er government – recognize this.

Biao Liu of Pu'er Coffee Association (a trade group) commented: "without Nestlé, we wouldn't have the coffee industry in Pu'er and Yunnan. After many of years hard work, local communities appreciate the Nestlé's efforts immensely. Their purchasing represents one-third of the total coffee production here." Technical executive Jiazhi Hou stated with a sense of self-satisfaction that "when we came in 1997, the majority of people still rode a bicycle to work. We see them become rich step-by-step, first buying motorbikes, then building villas and buying cars."

A small military airport in Pu'er, Si'mao airport, was converted for civil use in order to accommodate the high demand for transportation. This has significantly improved transportation between Pu'er and Kunming: 45 minutes by air compared with 5–6 hours by road (12 hours by road in 2002). There are three flights a day and every flight is almost full. Highway infrastructure has also greatly improved (there is little rail transport due to Yunnan's mountainous terrain).

Although the coffee market is growing, Nestlé still urges farmers not to "put all their eggs in one basket" by withdrawing from other cash crops such as Pu'er tea and tobacco. First, Pu'er tea has a long history and represents a long-standing local culture, which Nestlé intends to protect. Second, growing other cash crops diversifies investments and hedges the risks inherent in volatile markets, or those presented by natural disasters. It is not only advisable but feasible to grow tea and coffee in the same year, since the coffee harvest season begins in October and ends in February, and the tea harvest begins in March and ends in September. Though it is itself a purchaser, Nestlé teaches farmers to follow the market price and estimate the future prices and market trends in order to avoid unnecessary risks in trading. Nowadays, most farmers have learned to check the international coffee purchasing price online, and only sell at a reasonable procurement price. Farmers are free to sell to any buyers (e.g. Nestlé, Starbucks or De Hong Hou Gu) even if they are trained by Nestlé.

3.7.2 Supplier environmental management

Nestlé involves itself in environmental stewardship. For coffee producers, this means protection of primary forest and conservation of natural resources, including water, soil, energy and biodiversity.

Coffee processing pollutes water. Waste-water from the ferment-and-wash process is highly acidic. If the water is released into a farm field, it acidifies the soil, making it unsuitable for growing crops. After the ferment-and-wash process the beans must be rinsed again, producing more acidic waste-water. A new type of eco-processing equipment uses less water, and farmers are encouraged and trained by Nestlé to further treat waste-water. Nestlé provided two approaches, one for small farmers and another for large-scale growers and coffee companies. The company also advised farmers to plant more shade trees to prevent the coffee trees from producing too many cherries per annum, and to reduce water loss and soil erosion. Though sunshine encourages the trees to grow more cherries, too much will reduce the trees' long-term productivity.

Nestlé also requires farmers to minimize pesticides in coffee planting, and refuses to accept any coffee beans that test for more pesticide than is allowed by the 4C coffee standard. It was not easy to encourage farmers to implement these practices due to investment requirements and traditional growing customs. Nestlé accomplished this by continued persuasion and successful demonstrations of various coffee-growing techniques required by the 4C (at the demonstration farm).

The Common Code for the Coffee Community, also known as 4C,[3] offers voluntary, open, participatory guidance for sustainable practices for green coffee production, processing and trade. The 4C standards are not a certification but rather a verification of suppliers' environmental, social and economic performance. The

3   See http://www.4c-coffeeassociation.org.

pillars of 4C include a code of conduct, rules of participation for trade and industry, support mechanisms for farmers, a verification system and a participatory governance structure. The 4C Code of Conduct covers social, environmental and economic sustainability.

Nestlé addresses 4C with the Nescafé Plan[4] (Nescafé is the Nestlé subsidiary for coffee products worldwide). According to the plan, all directly purchased green coffee must meet 4C standards by the end of 2015. The Nescafé Plan has the support of the Rainforest Alliance and the 4C Association. In addition, 90,000 tonnes of Nescafé coffee will be sourced according to the Rainforest Alliance and Sustainable Agriculture Network (SAN) principles by 2020, about half of its total purchase.

Since 1980 governments and activists have focused on sustainable development as a way of integrating environmental and social considerations with traditional economic concerns. According to the World Commission on Environment and Development, sustainable development "meets the needs of the present without compromising the ability of future generations to meet theirs".[5] "The Nescafé Plan: Nestlé's Visionary Coffee Development, China" received the 2012 World Business and Development Awards (WBDA) for its efforts towards this goal, delivering both commercial success and helping to improve social, economic and environmental conditions by developing diverse coffee procurement initiatives in Yunnan.

4   See http://www.nestle.com/csv/case-studies/allcasestudies/thenescaf%C3% A9plan-mexico.

5   World Commission on Environment and Development. (1987). *Our Common Future*. New York: OUP.

3.8 Non-supply chain stakeholder engagement

Nestlé has a proactive policy towards natural resources in China, including access, use and protection of those resources. As Nestlé executive Jonathan Dong, said:

> we must align ourselves with the priorities of the central and local governments. To do this, we must have confidence in the government and that what the government does is right. China's economic growth proves the priorities they set are effective and right. To achieve alignment, there is a great need for internal and external lobby.

The central government's priorities are represented by the "San Nong" policies. The Pu'er local government's priority is to build Pu'er into China's coffee capital and make coffee an economic pillar. This is represented by the region's application to the Ministry of Agriculture for a national quality assurance centre and a coffee trading and production centre in Pu'er.

3.8.1 Engagement with central government and associated organizations

Because of its size, history and influence, Nestlé plays an important role in the determination and implementation of government policy and how the central government interacts with other relevant institutions, such as the Agricultural Ministry, China Beverage Industrial Association and China Agricultural University. Founded in 1993, the China Beverage Industrial Association (CBIA) deals with issues affecting the beverage industry and market. It acts as a conduit of information between the government and beverage makers, assisting implementation of government policies, industry analysis, and coordination among involved companies and organizations. The Agricultural University offers agriculture-related courses in business, economics, engineering and veterinary medicine, among other specialities. Its graduates work in business, government and agriculture. Nestlé shares information and course materials with the university and recruits employees from its alumni.

In effect, Nestlé's agricultural service office in Pu'er acts as a traffic manager, facilitating the flow of information between the coffee farmers, local coffee community and other organizations. For example, in May 2012, CBIA conducted a workshop for tea and coffee producers to encourage communication and information-sharing. Considering the amount of both tea and coffee in Pu'er, Nestlé proposed the workshop be held there and almost all the large tea and coffee companies attended.

3.8.2 Engagement with provincial and local government

Nestlé depends on the local government for its development in China and takes pains to align itself with regional and local objectives and priorities. When it decided to support the cultivation of coffee on a large scale, Nestlé knew it had to lobby the government because large farmlands in Pu'er were controlled by the local government and subject to local approval. In addition, Nestlé wanted to pursue a win–win strategy and balance its interests with those of the government and the farmers. When the global financial crisis hit in 2012, the market price for coffee slumped overnight, and the local government asked Nestlé to buy surplus beans above its original commitment at a protected price. Nestlé agreed, buying an additional 2,000 tonnes to satisfy the local government.

The Pu'er government encouraged Nestlé to work with the Pu'er Tropical Plant Institute (a higher educational institution) to set up a coffee lab, carrying out research, providing training to government officials and coffee company managers and offering coffee-related courses to undergraduate students, who are normally recruited by the coffee companies on graduation. Nestlé provided services normally provided by agricultural universities on coffee plantations, because coffee is not traditionally grown in China, and China's agricultural ministry and university do not possess the necessary knowledge.

Seeing the economic potential of the coffee industry, the Pu'er government set up a Pu'er coffee steering committee led by an administrative team, including the leaders of almost all of the city's administrative departments. The committee's objectives include setting industry policies and regulating, planning and serving the coffee industry in Pu'er. Its development strategy is to become a national exemplar city of a green economy.

Coffee is one of the economic pillars supporting that ambition.[6] Therefore the city intends to strengthen the coffee industry, including logistics and warehousing, deep processing (roasting and finished product processing) and promotion of local brands. The steering committee has a wide view of the entire coffee value chain and hopes to build Pu'er into not only a coffee capital in China but also an international coffee production destination. There is also a plan to build a national coffee R&D centre and a national lab (approved by the General Administration of Quality Supervision, Inspection and Quarantine of China.)

The Coffee Association of Yunnan includes coffee companies and farmers, with the goal of protecting local members' rights and interests. On occasion, Nestlé speaks on behalf of local farmers through the Association.

In 2012 Nestlé signed a Memorandum of Understanding (MoU) with the Pu'er government to double its coffee procurement in Yunnan over the following five years. The government and Nestlé agreed to step up cooperation, to include educating and training

6   The other economic pillars of Pu'er include tea, roast tobacco and tourism.

local farmers, providing technical support and accelerating a scientific plantation system in Pu'er. To this end, Nestlé is also building a Nescafé Coffee Centre, which consists of a coffee farming institute and consumer experience centre. Construction began in September 2015.

3.9 The final word

Nestlé's success is dependent on several factors, including its long-term vision of coffee procurement in Yunnan and its relationships with suppliers, the local government, various professional organizations and other stakeholders. Nestlé's business strategy includes the creation of shared value for all its stakeholders: suppliers, government, community, consumers and itself. In 2011, Nestlé introduced the Nescafé Plan, a global initiative which creates value across the coffee supply chain. As a pioneer in China, Nestlé had the vision to develop its business and improve the local coffee industry for long-term sustainable development. How it fares in the face of the evolving local market, increased competition and a volatile economy is a question Nestlé must answer every day.

Several international corporations now compete in the Chinese coffee market. McDonald's is rolling out a new McCafé format and adding coffee bars to some existing outlets. China Resources Enterprise Ltd, a Hong Kong-based company that currently operates 90 Pacific Coffee chains in Asia, has 1,000 new Chinese outlets in its pipeline. Costa Coffee, owned by Britain's Whitbread, is opening more than 250 new stores in the next three years, adding to its 180 existing outlets.

More importantly, Starbucks has arrived as a powerful competitor to Nestlé. Even though it does not currently buy or sell large volumes of beans or related products in Yunnan, it competes with an increasing number of coffee shops and some retail locations. In November 2010, Starbucks signed an agreement with the Yunnan provincial government to establish its first coffee farm in the province to ensure a stable supply. In the latter half of 2011, Starbucks acquired a 51% stake in a local coffee bean producer. In 2012 it signed an agreement to form a joint venture company with Ai Ni Group, an established agricultural company and coffee producer in Yunnan.

The venture, which is controlled by Starbucks, purchases and exports high-quality Yunnan Arabica beans, as well as operating dry mills in the province. Essentially, Starbucks is buying coffee beans from this corporation rather than individual farmers or farm groups. Starbucks is considering China as a potential second home market after the USA and will increase its store count in China to 1,500 in five years. In 2012 Starbucks opened a Farmer Support Centre in Yunnan, a seeming imitation of Nestlé's approach. The local Pu'er government warmly welcomed Starbucks to Pu'er with multiple intentions: to promote its reputation as China's coffee capital, to boost the local coffee economy and to encourage competition among foreign players.

In addition to the international brands, a few domestic coffee brands also compete for the Chinese coffee market. Local brands are supported by the government in some respects, including favourable regulations and government subsidies. Dehong Hogood Coffee, the first coffee supplier in Yunnan, announced in 2012 that it would phase out bean sales to Nestlé, ending a ten-year partnership between the two companies. The ending of the agreement saw the beginning of Chinese exports directly to the international market, rather than through an established coffee giant.

Furthermore, the Pu'er government hopes to develop its local coffee industry for export to the world, following the example of Jamaica's Blue Mountain Coffee. Yunnan is still far from competing with famous coffee regions in the world market, because exported coffee must meet stringent international requirements and standards. To reach this goal, Pu'er currently relies on Nestlé to help implement these standards and improve quality. Thus far, a few autonomous prefectures (自治州) have registered their local brands, such as Baoshan Coffee and Hongde Coffee, using a Protected Geographical Indication (PGI),[7] even though they have not distinguished themselves from other provincial coffees in terms of flavour or aroma. A PGI is a name or logo that identifies a product's place of origin (such as a town, region or country). In short, the local government wants to maximize the value of its coffee. While PGIs could help Yunnan build its name in the market, too many local brands will inevitably compete internally, thereby undermining the brand value of Yunnan coffee, driving down the price and diluting the value of the competing PGIs.

These are the main issues Nestlé, along with Yunnan's coffee producers, buyers and local governments, will need to address in the years to come.

3.10 Case summary

Global food producer Nestlé is just one of several food companies competing for the supply of coffee beans in Yunnan province. Rather than competing simply on price, Nestlé is building a three-way relationship with local farmers and also the local government, which wants to develop the coffee-farming economy and move further up the value chain. This case study examines how Nestlé:

---

7   See http://ec.europa.eu/agriculture/quality/schemes/index_en.htm.

- Procures its coffee beans, along with the workings of its Agricultural Service Team

- Engages with stakeholders, both farmers and government

- Develops the competences of its suppliers, helping farmers to develop their skills and improve quality

- Works with local government to help further the ambitions of the latter to move into coffee processing rather than just supply of raw beans

- Sets a premium on environmentally friendly coffee production, including encouraging farmers to use fewer chemicals and harmful fertilizers, and teaching local producers how to use less water and treat waste-water

- Supports local communities in order to strengthen the whole value chain, not just its own position

4
Sustainable practice in China: SKF

4.1 Introduction

SKF is a Swedish ball-bearing manufacturer founded in 1907. The company supplies products, solutions and services within rolling bearings, seals, mechatronics, services and lubrication systems to customers around the world.[1] Services include technical support, maintenance services, condition monitoring and training. SKF has been operating in China for over 100 years, and provides products and services to a variety of companies.

Rather than focus on any one partnership, this case study looks at a range of SKF initiatives. It begins with Pinghu Geothermal Energy Plant, and then looks at the partnership with Bao Steel, which is helping the customer to reduce CO_2 emissions. The focus then turns from manufacturing to supply chain management, and we will look at relationships with suppliers and focus on the introduction of a GSP (global standard palleting) system in China. This

1   See http://www.skf.com/group/our-company/index.html.

system of recycling pallets has also had a great impact on CO_2 emissions. Both individually and together, these initiatives show how SKF is working with other companies and with Chinese businesses to tackle sustainability issues on a variety of levels.

SKF's fundamental strength lies in its ability to continuously develop new technologies and then use those technologies to create products that offer competitive advantage to customers. SKF has achieved its capabilities by combining hands-on experience in over 40 industries with unique international knowledge across technology platforms: bearings and units, seals, mechatronics, services and lubrication systems.

Sustainability is one of the SKF group's five strategic drivers (the others are innovation, speed, quality and profitability). SKF further defines sustainability in terms of four "cares": business care, environmental care, employee care and community care.

The focus of SKF's technology development is on reducing the environmental impact of an asset during its life-cycle, in both the company's own operations and those of its customers.

In 2009 SKF started a programme called the "responsible sourcing programme". The central idea of this programme is to work with suppliers on responsible innovation and strengthen the adherence to the SKF Code of Conduct in the supply chain. As a starting point, SKF helps suppliers to comply with the SKF supplier code of conduct including environmental and social, health and safety responsibilities. As part of its responsible sourcing programme, SKF started off by requesting energy-intensive suppliers to report CO_2 emissions back to 2009. Today, SKF works to help all energy-intensive major suppliers apply for certification to the new energy management standard ISO 50001 by 2016, as a part of the Group's climate strategy. This will ensure a systematic implementation of sound energy management resulting in continual improvement.

4.2 SKF in China

In 2012, SKF celebrated 100 years of doing business in China. During a week of celebrations SKF China announced several initiatives. The first was the launching of the next phase of the re-manufacturing joint venture with Bao Steel (see below).[2] SKF also announced the establishment of a new campus in Jiading, Shanghai. The campus includes a new factory for wheel bearings for passenger cars, as well as relocation and expansion of the Global Technical Centre China, SKF Solution Factory and SKF College.

Third, SKF inaugurated its new bearing and truck hub unit factory in Jinan, Shandong Province.[3] The new factory is intended to support the continued growth of SKF's business in China and Asia more generally. Finally, SKF broke ground on a new state-of-the-art regional distribution centre equipped with green technology located in the Wai Gao Qiao Free Trade Zone in Shanghai. Both the new warehouse and the campus were operational at the end of 2013 and built to the LEED standard.[4]

---

2   Shanghai Bao Steel Group Corporation, commonly referred to as Bao Steel, is a state-owned iron and steel company headquartered in Shanghai, China (see http://www.baosteel.com). According to www.worldsteel.org, Bao Steel is the second-largest steel producer in the world (after ArcelorMittal) measured by crude steel output, with an annual output of around 20 million tonnes (China's total steel production in 2006 was 381.5 million tonnes). Bao Steel employs around 109,000 employees, has annual revenues of around US$21.5 billion and produces a mix of high-quality products.

3   According to the SKF glossary entries on ball-bearings and roller bearings, the main difference in the performance of these two bearing types is that ball-bearings have lower friction than roller bearings, while roller bearings have a higher load-carrying capacity.

4   Leadership in Energy and Environmental Design (LEED) consists of a suite of rating systems for the design, construction and operation of high-performance green buildings, homes and neighbourhoods.

To get a better understanding of SKF sustainable operations in China we met with Alicia Li, sustainability supervisor for SKF China. She explained the background to these initiatives:

> In mechanical manufacturing industries, Chinese suppliers traditionally are not as concerned about social responsibility as those in consumer goods manufacturing because they are in a B2B business and face lower risk to direct consumers. Especially in the initial stages of implementing these environmental, health, safety and social initiatives, it is difficult for them to understand and pay attention to this. During our own audits, we help them build a sustainable mind-set. This is the most important, but this mind-set may also take a very long time to build.

At the moment, rolling elements are normally sourced from overseas plants while inner and outer rings and cages are produced in China. However, SKF intends to localize components production in China. The SKF Global Technology Centre China is responsible for production line design, testing and new product development. One of the major issues for SKF operations in China, however, is energy consumption. Most electricity generated in China comes from coal-fired power stations. Rather than rely on these, SKF has turned for supply to two plants in Pinghu and Jinan that produce clean geothermal energy.

SKF received a government subsidy from Zhejiang for the construction of the Pinghu plant because, as Alicia Li said, "the government considered it a very good project for reducing energy consumption. The Pinghu plant in Zhejiang saved 13,000 kWh and reduced over 100 tonnes of CO_2 emissions in 2012."

4.3 Pinghu plant and geothermal energy

The construction of the first stage of the No. 1 factory at SKF Pinghu was finished in 2008. In August 2010 it expanded to include a heating, ventilation and air-conditioning (HVAC) system using geothermal air conditioning, the leading technique in green and energy-saving air conditioning.[5] Geothermal is the most environmentally friendly form of air-conditioning system, as it provides high efficiency, emits no pollution and has zero exhaust. The underground geo-exchanger where the energy is produced is a closed-loop system and therefore there is no physical exchange, only temperature exchange.

Geothermal air conditioning provides both heating and cooling utilizing underground resources. This system consists of geo-exchangers and heat pump units. In winter the geo-exchangers extract energy from underground and provide indoor heating through the heat pump units. The ground thus represents the heat source of the system. In summer the heat pump units collect indoor heat and release the energy underground through the geo-exchanger loops. Thus the ground becomes the cooling source of the heat pump units. The efficiency of the ground-source air pump is not influenced by extreme environment temperatures as the temperature underground is between 17°C and 18°C throughout the year. Energy consumption is 35–50% less than in fossil-fuel-powered systems.

In the first factory, centralized heat units were installed on three levels. Because of the unbalanced needs for heating and cooling within the factory, the system applied auxiliary dissipation methods

5   Wang, T., & Cheng, T. (2011). Air conditioning: carbon reduction in practice. *The Connection*, 24, 40. Retrieved from http://skf.elanders.cn/media/custom/upload/File-1343119784.pdf.

to make sure the ground was balanced. This method not only reduced the requirement of the geothermal system significantly but also ensured its long-term implementation with high efficiency. The system proved its efficiency during the hottest period of summer when the building stored a great deal of heat energy. The operational effect reached the specification requirements according to the design during a long period of high temperatures in 2011.

If SKF switches entirely to the geothermal system then, based on the analysis of Pinghu No. 1 factory, carbon production can be reduced by 162.66 tonnes per annum. According to the Geothermal Energy Association, the US environment office that evaluates geothermal systems, every 80 kW installation of geothermal systems equals the reduction of greenhouse gas exhaust from 12 cars, and the planting of trees covering 6,000 m^2 per year. According to these figures, the application of the first factory project of SKF China equates to the planting of trees over 16,000 m^2.

4.4 Re-manufacturing centre for Bao Steel

Asia accounts for almost 50% of the world steel market, compared with less than 30% a decade ago. China's share of the world bearing market is about 25%. The Chinese bearing market is rather fragmented, with the main international bearing manufacturers accounting for about one-third of the total market shares. These international players[6] include the Schaeffler Group,[7] Timken,[8]

---

6   See http://www.skf.com/group/investors/bearings-market.
7   See http://www.schaeffler.com/content.schaeffler.de/en/index.jsp.
8   See http://www.timken.com/en-us/products/bearings/Pages/default.aspx.

NSK,[9] NTN[10] and JTEKT.[11] Some of the largest domestic players include Wafangdian (ZWZ), Luoyang (LYC), Harbin (HRB), Zhejiang Tianma (TMB), Wanxiang Qianchao and C&U.

China is the largest producer and consumer of steel in the world. 2012 was a difficult year for an industry that saw its profits decline by nearly 96% in the first half of the year compared with the same period the previous year. According to the World Steel Association, about 50% of global steel production is used in the housing and construction sector, making it the biggest consumer of steel today. The global downturn and recent economic slowdown in China have dampened the construction industry in the world's largest nation. The consequent fall in steel demand has urged the Chinese steel industry to look for new ways to cut production costs. This is where SKF has its expertise.

The steel industry in China faces a number of challenges including high-energy consumption, pollution and complex production procedures.[12] Will Wang, General Manager of the Industrial Service Centre (ISC), more commonly called the re-manufacturing centre, and his colleagues have been working with one of China's largest steel producers, Bao Steel, for several years to reduce operational cost and pollution while maintaining the stable operation of key equipment. Bao Steel's original mind-set was that, once a bearing failed, it was regarded as useless and thrown away. SKF saw that practice as wasteful. A bearing's design life is much less than its working life. After failure, bearings can still probably be repaired. Repairing bearings reduces the cost to the customer, but equally

9   See http://www.nsk.com.
10   See http://www.ntn.co.jp.
11   See http://www.jtekt.co.jp.
12   SKF Annual Report 2012: financial, environment and social performance (p. 201), retrieved from http://www.skf.com/group/investors/reports/year-end-report-2012.

importantly it helps to reduce CO_2 emissions. SKF completely changed Bao Steel's mind-set on this issue. Thus, repairing bearings became a green service offered to Bao Steel.

4.5 Industrial Service Centre

According to Will Wang, the relationship between SKF and Bao Steel has gone through three stages. In the first stage, 20 years ago, Bao Steel's equipment was imported from Germany, France and Japan. The majority of the bearings in the equipment from Europe were manufactured by SKF. In this stage, the relationship was a transactional buyer–supplier relationship. Later, in the second phase, the demand for bearings produced by SKF increased. SKF then proposed that it should manage the inventory for Bao Steel. SKF calls this Trouble-Free Operation (TFO), while in the supply chain management literature it is known as vendor managed inventory (VMI). The location of the warehouse was also moved from outside to inside Bao Steel. In the third phase, SKF and Bao Steel signed a strategic partnership agreement in 2008. Through this agreement Bao Steel has learned advanced management knowledge and international development experience from SKF, while SKF can increase its market share in China through the collaboration with Bao Steel. SKF also started procuring steel from Bao Steel. Thus both firms are suppliers and customers to each other.

Bao Steel proposed the idea of an umbrella programme called "Green Bao Steel". SKF is now trying to align its products/service with Bao Steel's priorities and help the latter to improve its environmental efficiency.

As part of a strategic partnership agreement between SKF and Bao Steel, both jointly established an Industrial Service Centre (ISC)

May 2007	Joint venture establishment signing ceremony between SKF (China) Co. Ltd and Shanghai Baosteel Industry Technological Service Co. Ltd
May 2008	SKF Industrial Service (Shanghai) company inauguration ceremony
September 2009	SKF Industrial Service (Shanghai) company roll service inauguration ceremony
May 2010	High-level management conference between Baosteel and SKF held in the Swedish Pavilion at the Shanghai World Expo
August 2010	SKF ConRo signing ceremony between Baosteel and SKF

TABLE 4.1   ISC milestones

or re-manufacturing centre, with SKF holding 66% and Bao Steel 34% of the shares in 2008 (see Table 4.1). Both consider the ISC their own baby. Many employees of the ISC come from Bao Steel. The ISC is a financially independent organization and has around 130 employees with three functional departments (marketing and sales, technical solutions and production) in addition to the finance and HR departments. Since the ISC's establishment it has repaired 500 tonnes of bearings, which by April 2013 had reduced CO_2 emission by 3,000 tonnes.

The service process is very simple. Bearings that need repairing come from Bao Steel to the ISC, which is located near the steel company's plant. As explained by Xiaofeng Xu, Senior Technical Supporter of the ISC:

> We are responsible for diagnostics and repairing; this is coordinated by the strategic account department. After the repair, we provide diagnostic and repair results. The biggest difference between us and other companies is that in addition to repairs, we also provide on-site technical improvement advice.

SKF's re-manufacturing centre provides advice on how to improve Bao Steel's bearing performance. This brings SKF a competitive advantage. SKF provides economic advice and technical service on improving bearing performance at Bao Steel, which means that Bao Steel gets more value from SKF's service.

4.6 How SKF, Bao Steel and the ISC work

There are three business units within SKF: Regional Sales and Services (RSS), Strategic Industries and Automotive. There are also two departments interacting with Bao Steel: Strategic Account Management and the ISC, both of which belong to RSS. The former is responsible for selling new bearings to Bao Steel and the latter for repairing bearings. RSS contributes the largest amount of revenue (37%) to SKF.

Within Bao Steel there is an Industry Technological Service company, which is both the ISC's shareholder and its customer. This organization deals with end-users (production lines) and the Technical Solutions department, which is sometimes contracted by the end-users. Whenever a problem with bearings is identified, either the end-users or Technical Solutions will call the ISC to see if the bearing can be repaired. If not, the client will turn to Strategic Account Management to authorize the purchase of a new bearing. There is no competition between the ISC and Strategic Account Management. Both take a long-term view with the aim of adding value for the customer. Both exchange information and pass sales/repair needs to each other. It has been proposed that Strategic Account Management should be co-located with the ISC in order to better serve Bao Steel and enable better information exchange with the ISC.

The ISC is focused on the processes where bearings are used more extensively, such as continuous casting, hot rolling mill and cold rolling mill. The ISC provides a total solution service and business model for the bearings used in continuous casting, which means Bao Steel outsources this service completely to the ISC in exchange for a lump sum paid annually. SKF's caster roll service offers a complete professional solution including analysis, disassembling, testing, repairing and installation of caster roll lines and bearing reconditioning. The re-manufacturing centre is the only facility which repairs Bao Steel bearings, which come from various suppliers. This means that 90% of the re-manufacturing centre's revenue – a total of RMB 70 million in 2012 – is contributed by Bao Steel.

In addition to improving the reliability of continuous casters and extending their service life by 15%, SKF also helps Bao Steel increase process efficiency, reducing environmental impact as well as overall costs by 20%. This is an example of what SKF calls "knowledge engineering". This is beneficial to SKF too, as the longer the service life and more reliable the bearing is, the more cost-efficient it is for SKF. This business model makes it easier for the advanced technology to be injected into Bao Steel's production.

Another important function of the re-manufacturing centre is to serve as a collector of sales and market information for new product design at Bao Steel. The SKF R&D team collaborates with the Global Technical Centre China at Bao Steel to develop innovations and improvements.

4.7 SKF working with suppliers

SKF China believes that managing sustainability in the demand chain is just as important as managing quality or cost. There are several reasons for this. First, employees wish to work for responsible companies; second, this strategy could help protect brand image; third, it supports company values; and fourth, it creates competitive advantages for the company.

According to SKF's supplier code of conduct, SKF's suppliers and subcontractors also contribute to the company's brand image. Consequently, SKF expects its suppliers and subcontractors to

Box 4.1: The main features of SKF's supplier development practice

- Supplier quality development:
  - Supplier qualification
  - Supplier quality development – if potential suppliers cannot meet the qualification requirement
  - Supplier partnership programme, global major supplier database
- Supplier sustainability development:
  - SKF code of conduct for suppliers and subcontractors
  - Chinese version
  - Mail it to all suppliers
  - Major suppliers need to develop their own code of conduct
  - Over 50 SKF code of conduct audits (some carried out by a third party) in both 2012 and 2013 in China
  - Promote reduction of energy consumption and CO_2 report
  - 100% group major supplier reported CO_2 in 2008
  - 100% major suppliers to report CO_2
  - 100% of the energy-intensive major suppliers ISO 50001 certified in 2016 including seven suppliers in China

demonstrate the same high standards as does SKF itself (see Box 4.1). When working with suppliers, SKF measures their performance across five dimensions: quality, cost, delivery, innovation and management (QCDIM). By meeting these standards and fulfilling the requirements of SKF's supplier code of conduct, suppliers and subcontractors contribute to SKF's strong brand image.

SKF's supplier development practices have two distinct features: supplier quality development and supplier sustainability development. All suppliers are required to hold supplier qualifications, and only qualified suppliers can be involved in the "supplier partnership

Box 4.2: External recognition

SKF has received widely positive feedback from external experts and industry benchmarks over the years.

- In September 2014, SKF was included in the Dow Jones Sustainability Index for the 15th consecutive year. The assessment of the company's supply chain management has been among the best in the industry sector for several years.

- SKF has also been included for 14 years in the FTSE4Good and Ethibel PIONEER and Ethibel EXCELLENCE Investment Registers – both ethical investment stock market indices.

- Since 2012, SKF has worked with WWF Climate Savers. Climate Savers is a global WWF platform to engage business and industry on energy and climate. Companies in the Climate Savers set industry-leading strategies and targets to mitigate climate change.

Source: http://www.worldwildlife.org/partnerships/climate-savers.

programme" and be entered into the SKF global preferred supplier database. Supplier sustainability development includes the sustainable practices written into the SKF supplier code of conduct and disseminated to all the suppliers. Some of the major suppliers then develop their own codes of conduct to further disseminate learning to their own suppliers. Supplier sustainability development also includes ISO 14001 certificates, and energy and CO_2 emission reports.

When selecting suppliers, SKF sends specialist auditors to audit quality and separately to audit conformance to the code of conduct. Once suppliers are code-of-conduct approved, they are then audited biennially. SKF uses its own staff instead of third-party auditors, says Anders Lidholm, Global Responsible Purchasing Manager for the SKF Group, because "we want to be closer to our suppliers, we are more personal with suppliers and more focused on the suppliers' positive development than focusing on finding fault and punishing people".

From the beginning of 2007, SKF required its major first-tier suppliers to provide data on CO_2 emissions. A dedicated project was set up, the "IC supply chain", which set out to ascertain the amount of suppliers' CO_2 emissions as a percentage of SKF's total CO_2 emissions. In 2012, SKF China required CO_2 emission-intensive suppliers to to work towards ISO 50001 certification.[13] The project also changed its name to "responsible demand chain", and started to include health and safety and social aspects of responsibility as well.

To better implement the supplier development strategy a dedicated organizational structure, the Responsible Sourcing Committee (RSC), was set up. Committee members include the group demand chain director, corporate sustainability director, supplier quality development director, and responsible purchasing manager at SKF Global. The Committee meets several times a year.

Going beyond audit and shifting the focus to supplier compliance, SKF China also started working closely with suppliers to provide innovative products and services to its customers. One initiative is the "supplier innovation workshop", held for the first time in China in September 2013. Selected suppliers based in China and north-east Asia were invited in April to propose innovation ideas on

---

13   ISO 50001 is a specification created by the International Organization for Standardization (ISO) for an energy management system. The standard specifies the requirements for establishing, implementing, maintaining and improving an energy management system, whose purpose is to enable an organization to follow a systematic approach in achieving continual improvement of energy performance, including energy efficiency, energy security, energy use and consumption. The standard aims to help organizations continually reduce their energy use, and therefore their energy costs and their greenhouse gas emissions.

which they would like to collaborate with SKF for future implementation. Suppliers were told in advance that the conference not only aimed to persuade them to cut their costs, but also to encourage them to put forward proposals for products or services with a more environmentally friendly focus, and to offer suggestions on ways to reduce total supply chain costs. In the initial screening, 80 suppliers proposed more than 200 suggestions. SKF selected 15 suppliers with 20 suggestions for the final presentation and discussion. This event lasted for two days. The most suitable ideas were proposed by the workshop for further actions with related SKF technical centres and business units.

The final session of the workshop began with SKF technical teams and business units presenting their requirements, business excellence methods and tools. Suppliers were then divided into four groups based on the supply chains they were in. Each group comprised suppliers, SKF partners such as manufacturing plants, SKF application engineers (who were familiar with the relevant industry), SKF technical centre staff and SKF business excellence facilitators. Groups discussed proposals relating their impacts to upstream or downstream firms, whether the proposals were practical and feasible and whether they fulfilled the technical standards. Comments were considered from other group members. Finally each group reached agreement and presented its two best ideas on what SKF should do and how they would cooperate in a supply chain.

Vincent Yang, Purchasing Director at SFK China, said:

> there are two highlights of this workshop: the first one is that it is highly interactive and suppliers played a key and proactive role in the process. They talked most of the time and told us what they could offer and what we should do. The second highlight is that they were divided into groups based on their supply chains, so they are not on their own or acting

individually but coordinated and acting together, to optimize the whole chain rather than suboptimizing individual points.

He is optimistic about the future:

> We want to turn the workshop into an annual event. This year is just the first time, but suppliers know that we would like to hear their voices, and they now know how to do it better next time. I am sure the quality and effectiveness of next year's conference will be even better since everyone now knows its importance to a better degree. Our aim by 2016 is to have at least three to five products developed per proposal originating from suppliers.

Suppliers and SKF internal partners at the workshop also gave positive feedback. One general manager from a major supplier said, "In the past we were only asked to copy what SKF created; today we are very happy and honoured to sit down with SKF side by side to discuss how to create something new." GTCC (Global Technical Center China) manager Helen Bao said that "we are willing to assign project managers and lab capacities to work on some of the ideas that came out of this event." The final proposals were divided into cost proposals, high-potential product performance proposals and so on, and sent to different internal departments for further evaluation. All suppliers will be informed of the outcomes and further actions.

4.8 SKF GSP operational management

The SKF logistics service mainly serves the company's internal customers, SKF plants and sales companies. Within the SKF logistics department there are four core business areas: packaging, transportation, warehousing and supply planning. As Mike Fan, manager of

SKF Logistics China, explained, "We charge them for our services such as picking up containers and warehousing. We have prices for all our services. We treat our sales companies and plants as our customers. We do business development and provide customer services." Mike Fan joined the logistics department in 2006 when it was established, and has been in charge of packaging since the first day of service establishment.

For outbound flow (i.e. distribution of finished products), plants use SKF logistics services since the plants are not in charge of sales and marketing; at SKF, these are the responsibility of the sales companies. All products transported to sales companies have to go through the SKF logistics computer system, and thus the plants are unable to use third-party logistics services. However, for inbound flow such as raw materials or semi-finished items sourcing, the plants are free to choose their own way and have to manage by themselves. SKF logistics normally gives the plants a solution proposal for inbound services and waits to see if they accept the offer. Mike Fan continues, "for finished products, plants are not our customers. Once manufactured, the products are delivered to sales companies. So our customers would be sales companies."

SKF's internal sales companies face towards external customers. Plants are responsible for manufacturing, and sales companies are in charge of the end customers. Sales companies are only responsible for the local market. Overseas sales are organized between the plants, but the products will finally go to sales companies overseas. The plants do not deal directly with the end customer.

To address environmental requirements, when delivered to customers, 85–90% of SKF's bearings use GSP (global standard pallet) packaging. As Mike Fan explains, "No matter where the packaging suppliers are, we have a common requirement which is that the GSP you supply to me has to be the same standard." This means that, for example when the packaging is recycled, the trays could be made in China, the hoardings could be from Germany and the lids may be from India or Italy. Notwithstanding the origin of the packaging and the suppliers, SKF logistics services ensure that the packaging is the same size, can be assembled freely and, most importantly, recycling and reuse are not restricted by different suppliers.

The SKF "pallet pool system" has two main purposes: to reduce the purchase of new packaging to save costs, and to reduce transportation costs. SKF has customers in several different industries, and the company delivers its bearings to clients all over China. Thus, SKF built many hubs to gather all its GSPs and then send them to the pallet pool station jointly to save on transportation costs. Currently, SKF has pallet pools in Shanghai, Wuxi, Dalian and Jinan. There are plans to build another pallet pool in Chongqing or Zhenzhou. The purpose of pallet pools is to store, clean and repair the recycled pallets and then distribute them to customers. SKF also has hubs in Tianjin, Beijing, Dalian, Chongqing, Xian and Guangzhou.

SKF also has an automotive department, one of the three largest departments in the company. The pallets' return rate in the automotive department has reached almost 98%. Mike Fan says:

> The reason we can achieve this is that we have a deposit refund system. Under this system, all our customers must pay a deposit to us to get any of our GSP. And the amount of the deposit is far more than the total price of the GSP.

To illustrate, let us take a hypothetical example. Supplier A supplies bearing rings to one of SKF's plants. In the contract, supplier A would be required to use SKF's GSP to pack their bearing rings. While the GSP are all from SKF's pallet pool station, the figures in the SKF logistic services computer system will show how many pallets go out and come in. So suppliers cannot purchase GSP by themselves – they have to take the packaging from SKF directly.

If one GSP costs SKF RMB 30, the deposit SKF logistic services will ask for would be doubled to RMB 60. After the bearing rings are delivered to the SKF plant, the plant will refund the RMB 60 deposit to supplier A. However, if GSPs are damaged, no deposit will be refunded. This is a highly motivating and very simple system which ensures a high return rate for the standard pallets.

SKF also has a "pallet pool handling fee" (PPHF). For example, SKF logistic services might refund RMB 55 instead of RMB 60 to the plants. This way SKF will pay the pallet pool handling fee. Mike Fan explains:

> For plants, the cheapest packaging they can find costs at least RMB 30. However, we only charge them RMB 5 for packaging. Actually we are helping plants to save their costs. So, they are pleased to use our packaging system.

To illustrate further, a sales company sells 300 units of packaging to customers. SKF logistics services will help to store the products and deliver them to the customers. SKF logistics will charge for warehousing and take the delivery fees. Simultaneously, SKF logistics will also charge the sales company the deposit for those 300 GSPs. The sales company will be responsible for recycling those GSPs from the customers. Then, SKF logistics will refund RMB 55 back to the sales company after deducting the PPHF. This way, there are deposits in each stage in the process. Everyone who pays the deposit will carefully look after the GSPs and try to return them to the logistics department in the best condition.

For the sake of security, SKF logistics will charge PPHF to both the plants and sales company. For SKF logistics there are two different flows. One is the inbound flow for plants and the other is the outbound flow for the sales company. For each flow, SKF logistics will charge deposit and handling fees. SKF China took over the handling fee system from SKF global practice. Before the SKF

China logistics department was founded, the handling fee system had been running in Europe and had been in existence for around 30 to 40 years.

If a pallet is broken, SKF will inspect and determine if it can be repaired. The department will try its best to repair and reuse any pallet. However, if a pallet is no longer usable, SKF has a green process for handling the breakage. SKF scraps the company's logo and then hands the broken pallet over to qualified low-carbon companies for recycling.

Mike Fan concludes: "From my point of view, if the deposit refund system and pallet pool station have been well-managed, we have achieved 80 or 90% of our targets." SKF employs only two people in the packaging department; operation of the pallet pools has been outsourced. Each factory has one person working with SKF GSP. The outsourcing company provides the manpower and SKF pays their salaries. Additionally, at the warehouse, there is also a person responsible for helping SKF logistics with cleaning the pallets and delivering GSPs to the customers according to the accepted orders. As Mike Fan says:

> The packaging suppliers deal with our packaging every day, so they are quite familiar with SKF's standards. When they repair the packaging, they are clear about the level of standards we want. If another supplier is used, we have to teach them what standards we expect and the repair work, i.e. which one could be repaired and to what extent the repairable part of the packaging may be maintained. Our current supplier is very clear about our requirements. Their workers are all skilled and adept. It is an easier way for us.

4.9 The final word

Tom Johnstone, SKF's President and CEO, succinctly explained what SKF is trying to achieve when he introduced the company's 2013 annual report:

> The initiatives which we are driving in SKF and the actions they are taking to address cost and strengthen growth give us a strong foundation to build on during this year and into the coming years. SKF has put in place priorities to drive our business going forward and during the year we made significant progress. These priorities are built around SKF Care – our strategy for sustainability. This Annual Report is also built around SKF Care and the four dimensions of Business Care, Environment Care, Employee Care and Community Care.

4.10 Case summary

Ball-bearing manufacturer SKF has long been a leader in its industry in terms of both quality and sustainability. In China, SKF has introduced practices which have benefited not only the company itself but also its customers, particularly in areas such as energy saving and waste reduction. SKF has set a benchmark for the entire steel industry in China. Important practices introduced by SKF include:

- Innovative new systems for energy use and conservation such as the nonpolluting HVAC system of geothermal air conditioning

- Repair and re-manufacture of ball-bearings in order to reduce costs and CO_2 emissions

- Introducing a reusable packaging system, the global standard pallet, again with the aim of reducing costs and CO_2 emissions

- Organizing and leading supplier innovation workshops to spread best practice among other companies

- Creating a change of mind-set and approach to sustainability on the part of one of SKF's major customers, Bao Steel

5
On the "Road to Zero": Sony

5.1 Introduction

Sony Corporation was founded in Tokyo in 1946 by a group of entrepreneurs including two of the most famous figures in Japanese business history, Ibuka Masaru and Morita Akio. Part of their purpose in establishing the business in the immediate aftermath of the Second World War was to help contribute to society and rebuild the Japanese economy. From this small beginning came today's Sony, which at the end of 2014 had 131,700 members of staff worldwide and consolidated sales and operating revenue of 7.7 trillion yen. Sony produces audio and video equipment, televisions, information and communications technology, semiconductors and electronic components.

Along with the strong social principles that have characterized the company from its inception, Sony also recognizes that its business activities have direct and indirect impact on the environment. As a result of this, Sony has set out an Environmental Vision, the goal of which is a "zero environmental footprint" by 2050. In order to turn the dream of a sustainable society into reality, Sony has set up a detailed environmental management plan and management system. This case study examines Sony's "Road to Zero", with particular emphasis on China. The 12th Five-Year Government Plan of China (2011–15) has a strong focus on energy saving, and also on climate change and other environmental issues. In this case study we shall see how Sony has responded to these issues during this period by focusing on green supply chain management, reduction of greenhouse gas emissions and the introduction of green products.

5.2 A glimpse into the corporate environmental management system

In April 2010 Sony launched its "Road to Zero" environmental plan. This plan had four key environmental aspects: climate change, resource conservation, chemical substances management and biodiversity conservation. Sony also set out in detail how it intended to realize the integrated "zero environmental footprint" in those four key environmental areas. In order to achieve its targets by the end of 2015, Sony set specific goals for each stage in the product life-cycle. Specifically, Sony has set quantified targets in whole key stages including product planning and design, procurement, operations, logistics and recycling.

5.3 Sony in China

In line with the entire Sony Group, Sony China has set its own targets.[1] These new targets were set when Sony achieved the targets

1   In 1996 Sony set up a wholly owned foreign enterprise (WOFE), Sony (China) Ltd based in Beijing, to coordinate and manage all business activities in China. The main purposes of this company are investing in information systems, market development and after-sales services, and coordinating

set out in the "Green Management 2010" midterm environmental plan, including a reduction of more than 30% in global CO_2 emissions across its business sites (compared with 2000 fiscal levels). In 2014, Sony reported that absolute GHG emissions were down 46% from the fiscal year 2000.

Since 1998, Sony has formulated uniform environmental midterm targets that encompass its operations around the world, and has revised these targets every few years. The "Green Management 2010" midterm environmental plan was introduced by Sony to reduce the company's environmental impact over five years during fiscal years 2006 to 2010. At the end of fiscal year 2009, Sony formulated "Green Management 2015", a set of midterm targets that serve as a yardstick for the environmental activities of Sony Group companies and divisions worldwide until the end of fiscal year 2015.

Sony also joined the WWF Climate Savers programme in 2006. Through the Climate Savers programme, Sony has established targets for reducing annual energy consumption and absolute emissions of the greenhouse gases. Progress towards these targets is monitored by WWF.

5.3.1 Sony China targets for Green Management 2015

The "Road to Zero" plan includes midterm environmental targets that are set applying backcasting methods. The plan includes specific targets across four perspectives through the entire product life-cycle. The environmental vision is Sony's aim to achieve a zero environmental footprint throughout Sony's business activities and product life-cycle by 2050. Table 5.1 shows some of the activities and targets that have been set.

───────────────────────────────

and managing business activities across affiliated companies in China. Sony China intends to create a comprehensive platform incorporating product planning, design, R&D, sales and services.

Research and development	• Actively concentrate on R&D investment in environmental energy. • Cooperate with Chinese research organizations to develop environment-related technologies.
Product planning and design	• Reduce annual average energy consumption by 30% from the 2008 level (achicved). • Strive to achieve energy conservation evaluation values on Chinese energy-saving standard products. • Reduce average weight per product by 10% from 2008 levels. • Continue to promote chemical substances management based on Management Regulations for Environment-related Substances to be controlled which are included in Parts and Materials (SS-00259: established by Sony on 29 March 2002; now in its tenth revision).
Procurement	• Establish a mechanism for determining suppliers' greenhouse gas emissions. • Conduct biodiversity assessments at resource extraction and harvesting sites.
Operations	• Reduce greenhouse gas emissions by an absolute value of 30% from 2000 levels. • Achieve an absolute reduction in the total volume of water used by 30% from 2000 levels. • Achieve an absolute reduction in waste from sites of 50% from 2000 levels. • Factories and offices across China to carry out annual regional environmental contribution activities that respond to the needs of local communities.
Logistics	• Reduce CO_2 emissions created by logistics by 14% from 2008 levels. • Reduce waste from packaging for incoming parts by 16% from 2008 levels.
Take-back and recycling	• Work with recycling factories to develop recycling systems. • Continue to design products that are easy to recycle.

TABLE 5.1   Sony China targets for Green Management 2015

Source: Sony China 2011 CSR Report.

Sony China is expected to play a major role in achieving the overall environmental goals of the Sony Group. First, production facilities in China are an important part of the Sony Group (eight manufacturing facilities out of 50 globally), and these plants contribute a significant amount of the company's total CO_2 emissions. Second, the green products manufactured and sold in China have a significant influence on Sony Group's global environmental

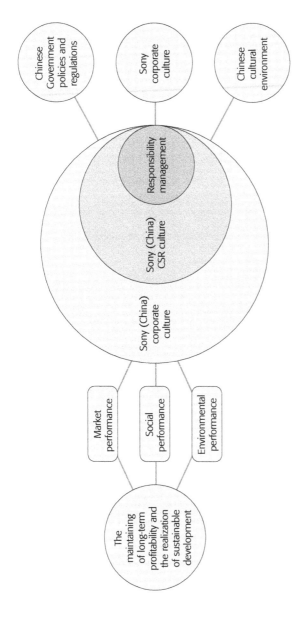

FIGURE 5.1 Sony China's CSR model

Source: Sony China 2011 CSR Report.

strategy. China is the second biggest market after the USA and before Japan. By the end of 2005 Sony had acquired integrated ISO 14001 certification for all its manufacturing plants in China. Third, China represents a major supply base for Sony. Finally, Sony China collaborates with Chinese research institutions to co-create environmental solutions, and therefore becomes a major source of innovative products.

While working together with other companies to develop a common framework of Corporate Social Responsibility (CSR) performance, Sony China is also seeking to introduce CSR procurement, namely, CSR management programmes throughout the supply chain that include legal compliance, employment, occupational health and safety, and environmental protection. Figure 5.1 shows this model in detail.

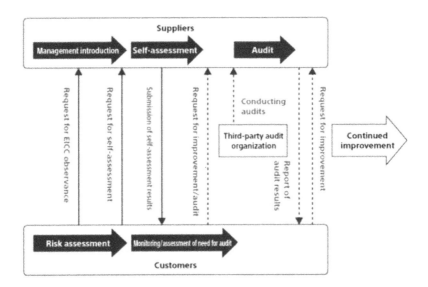

FIGURE 5.2   EICC framework

Source: http://www.sony.net/SonyInfo/csr_report/sourcing/supplychain/.

The Electronic Industry Citizenship Coalition (EICC) was established in 2004 with the aim of improving CSR performance in the electronics supply chain (see Figure 5.2 for details). Sony, as one of the member companies, participates in the activities of the EICC. In 2006, Sony China informed all its suppliers about the Sony supplier code of conduct, which is centred on the premise that since suppliers are engaged in the manufacture of Sony products, they should adhere to the Code and comply with Sony's standards. As part of its effort to assess compliance with the Code, Sony has introduced self-assessment questionnaires and briefing meetings. Some of Sony's suppliers have also been selected to undergo audits based on EICC standards. Sony requests all potential new suppliers to comply with the Code. If the existing suppliers don't pass the

As an integrated part of Sony Group	As a multinational corporation operating in China	As an enterprise pursuing outstanding performance	As a company aiming at achieving sustainable operation
• Follow Sony Group code of conduct, strategy, policy • Reflect Sony Group's standard requirements and actions • Implement best practice in reflecting the group's principles in China	• Follow "rooted in China", long-term development principle • Consider the background of China promoting sustainable development • Pay attention to key areas of social responsibility in China • Meet local requirements and adapt to local features	• Integrate CSR management into the whole business processes including procurement, product design, manufacturing, sales and marketing and services • Integrate CSR principles into Sony's culture • Align CSR practice with overall strategy and business operations	• Pay attention to and respond to the hot global CSR topics • Establish forward-looking and long-term CSR planning

TABLE 5.2   Sony China's principles of CSR practice

renewal audit, Sony asks the supplier to take corrective actions and report back on progress until full compliance has been achieved. Sony China's principles of CSR practice are shown in Table 5.2.

In 2004, Sony China established a Regional Environmental Office (REO) as a branch of HQ Environmental Affairs Department (a functional development). Its main responsibility is to manage and audit all environmental affairs in China, including guiding and auditing the implementation of Sony Group guidelines and directions, collecting China's regional environmental information and updates on Chinese environmental regulation so that headquarters can formulate suitable environmental policy and guidelines. The REO also works with other corporate functions including product quality, customer satisfaction, occupational health and safety and disaster prevention in order to achieve an effective environmental management system.

5.4 Green supply chain management

The product and service quality of suppliers and subcontractors are closely associated with that of Sony. Strict control of potentially hazardous chemical substances in the hundreds or thousands of parts in each of Sony's electronic products is critical in preventing environmental pollution. With the aim of encouraging suppliers to introduce green environmental management systems, Sony China has promoted the Sony Green Partner Environmental Quality Approval Program, which began in 2002. So far, over 1,000 local suppliers have become Sony Green Partners and their products now meet the most advanced and strict environmental requirements. This assists these suppliers when seeking international business in markets such as Europe where environmental standards are very high, and has a positive impact on the local environment.

The "Green Partner" programme was introduced in 2002 to ensure that Sony only procures from green partners who have successfully passed the audit. Sony's suppliers in China are audited by Sony each year to ensure that their environmental management systems are working properly. Sony was one of the first companies to introduce this system, which has now been adopted by other large corporations around the world.

In 2010, Sony China implemented a reform proposal, which put the renewal audit (i.e. auditors make decisions on whether to renew the membership for the "Green Partner" or not) into one factory. This project has played a significant role in promoting the Sony Green Partner Standards, especially in optimizing the allocation of audit resources and stabilizing audit quality. In 2010 Sony China also conducted an investigation of 332 companies supplying eight Sony plants in China. Among those suppliers, 61 were new suppliers and 271 suppliers were reviewed under the renewal audit. The result

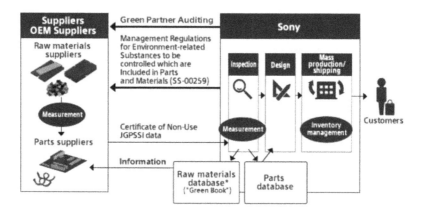

FIGURE 5.3   System for managing chemical substances in products

Source: http://www.sony.net/SonyInfo/csr_report/environment/chemical/products/index2.html.

of the investigation indicated that all the suppliers complied with Sony supplier code of conduct.

Sony China also applies Sony's global standards for the management of chemical substances when procuring raw materials and parts (see Figure 5.3). In China Sony complies strictly with the Chinese government's "Management Methods on the Pollution Control of Electronic Information Products". By applying the Green Partner Environmental Quality Approval Program, Sony makes sure that manufactured products do not contain harmful chemical substances. Meanwhile, the Green Partner programme helps partners to improve their own environmental management practices.

5.5 The green product life-cycle

5.5.1 Green supply chain and logistics

In order to reduce impact on the environment during the transportation of products, Sony strives continually to improve packaging, modes of transportation and transportation efficiency.

Sony Supply Chain Solutions (Shanghai) has worked with product design, manufacturing and other departments to provide lightweight product manuals, high-strength lightweight packaging materials and smaller boxes. Sony China has also introduced and expanded the use of "milk runs", regular round trips to collect or deliver goods. Products and parts are collected by Sony's own vehicles and transported following the best-designed routes to Sony's sites. This significantly reduces the number of transport vehicles and their mileage. These vehicles are equipped with advanced GPS in order to keep track of their condition, select the best transportation routes, measure punctuality and make accurate pick-ups and deliveries.

On supply management, Sony China explains, "We have a set of criteria for selecting suppliers. In particular, we select suppliers from a sustainable development perspective. We periodically audit our suppliers on-site and monitor the production environment of our suppliers." Sony China also collaborates continuously with its suppliers: "We are a leader in terms of managing the chemical substances in our products. We were also the first to set up the green partners system. Many companies have learned from us and introduced similar systems."

Sony China organizes an annual suppliers' conference, at which the company educates its suppliers on environmental issues in order to achieve the common goal of "zero environmental footprint". As Sony China sees it:

> If we only send our suppliers a notice or a set of standards without explaining them, it is difficult for them to implement. The solution we adopted was not to ask our suppliers [to do it] but to do it with our suppliers together. This happens in two ways. Firstly, we communicate with the top management of our suppliers. Secondly, we educate top management and other responsible individuals about our standards, including on-site education. Our suppliers have been very cooperative.

The green partnership programme has been integrated into the procurement procedure. Each supplier is looked after by a particular Sony plant, which normally educates the supplier concerned.

5.5.2 Green products

Sony strives to minimize the impact on the environment through product research and design. Through technology innovation, Sony continues to improve product energy efficiency and actively looks for alternatives to hazardous materials to minimize the use of hazardous substances, minimize the consumption of plastic, metal and glass and promote the application of renewable materials and recyclable materials.

To achieve the best energy-saving performance in the industry, Sony considers how to reduce the impact of its products on the environment right from the product planning and design phase. For example, in 2011 the new Bravia LCD TV continued the Bravia brand's philosophy, which has consistently focused on environmental protection. In that year, the number of low energy consumption LED product lines was expanded from 20 to 26. As Ann Wu of Sony says:

> The Bravia LCD TV has many energy-saving functions such as movement detection sensors, which can detect movements of either one person or several people within a certain distance from the TV. If one moves away from the screen or stops moving, e.g. when falling asleep, it will shut off the TV and cut off the power automatically. As a result, energy is saved. In addition, if you turn off the older TVs, a small amount of electricity is still consumed while it is plugged in. However, for the Bravia TV, even if you don't unplug, the electricity consumption is nearly zero.

This technology is very effective for energy saving. Some high-end models contain motion sensors that could automatically restore to ECO (eco mode) setting according to changes in human movement. For example, when the motion sensor detects no human movement, the sensor will switch off the power in order to save energy.

5.6 Reducing greenhouse gas emissions at sites

Sony's carbon reduction is managed throughout the life-cycle of Sony's products and business processes, ranging from technology research, product design, procurement, manufacturing, logistics and customer usage to the recycling of waste products. All of Sony's business units in China have been involved in carrying out energy-efficient facilities improvements, building a special energy-saving platform and promoting the best energy-saving initiatives. Through these efforts Sony China aims to reduce greenhouse emissions and achieve its 2015 targets. In June 2015, Sony reported that it expected to achieve these targets, and established its "Green Management 2020" plan, focusing on 30% less energy consumption in its electronics, efforts to work with supply chain partners on reducing their GHG emissions, and accelerating the use of renewable energy.[2]

In order to reach these targets Sony China conducts energy-saving assessments and improvements and has built special environmental communication platforms to share energy-saving initiatives and actively promote energy monitoring. This includes the management and replacement of air-conditioning units, energy-efficient lighting, construction of new environment friendly buildings and the upgrading of production equipment. Through these efforts, Sony strives to reduce greenhouse emissions.

- Since 2008, many Sony sites in China have been reducing energy consumption by air-conditioning units by replacing their R22 refrigerants with R418A. This has resulted in a combined reduction of 620 tonnes in CO_2 emissions.

- Sony continues to promote the installation of high-efficiency inverters at its sites in China. In 2010, as well as adding inverter controls to its existing chiller pump systems, Sony Electronics Huanan installed a single new energy-efficient inverter chiller unit. Together, these measures are expected

2   See http://www.sony.net/SonyInfo/News/Press/201506/15-051E/index.html.

to support a reduction of 780 tonnes in the company's annual CO_2 emissions.

The Chinese market offers many strategic opportunities for Sony to implement its strategy of sustainable innovation. China has had a stable political and economic environment, progressive economic policy and a more receptive society (especially after the Green Olympic Games of 2008 in Beijing). Moreover, the Chinese government has begun to emphasize CO_2 emission reduction since the 11th Five-Year Plan (2006–10). Now China is implementing the 12th Five-Year Plan and environmental protection is more important than ever. China's economy is also growing at a fast pace. Public ability and willingness to pay for goods has increased as people have more disposable income. The rapid development of technology creates more opportunities for Sony in areas such 3D technology, tri-network integration and high-speed mobile telephone networks.

5.7 The final word

Since the beginning of its operations in China, Sony has focused on contributing to China's CO_2 emission reduction programme. Sony aims to improve its operational efficiency and profitability through implementing innovative solutions. In China, consumers, NGOs and the media have started to pay more attention to corporate CO_2 emission. Sony China aims to continue its efforts and further contribute to building a culture of environmental protection in Chinese society.

There are also major challenges for Sony in China. For example, inferior counterfeit products infringe Sony's brand and harm brand equity and market share. The possibility that the renminbi might appreciate has also affected Sony's plans for business expansion in China. Labour costs in the country are rising. Pressure to protect the environment and manage resources is increasing, but the rules are rarely enforced.

The real situation in China is that "neither Customs houses nor State Administration for Industry and Commerce of the People's Republic of China is responsible for the monitoring and enforcement of environmental laws and regulations", according to Anna Wu, a Regional Environment Office Supervisor, Operations Platform Group at Sony. Locally, regulations are often not administered equally in terms of monitoring and enforcement. Foreign companies are often "the only focus of monitoring", or in other words, domestic players are treated more lightly.

At the same time, the Chinese central government started to pay more and more attention to the environmental issues and made policies in *all industries* helping companies improve their environmental protection systems. However, environmental solutions require investment, and sometimes do not produce returns immediately. Thus it is difficult for many companies (including Sony) to implement innovative solutions in an arena where Chinese companies compete on low-cost production.

Along with the financial issues, there are administrative and structural impediments as well. For example, the market for power supply hasn't been deregulated, which means that there is no financial incentive for Sony China to implement such projects related to renewable energy. In Japan, Sony's plants have their own power generators generating electrical power and are connected to the national grid. In China it is impossible to connect to the National Grid of China, but these innovative energy efficiency solutions helped reduce the company's energy bills and were especially helpful for certain areas of China where there is a lack of electricity.

5.8 Case summary

Sony has responded to the 12th Five-Year Plan with its "Road to Zero" programme in China, part of the Sony Group's larger vision of zero environmental footprint by 2050. Sony China is an important part of the group, and Sony sees success in China as instrumental to its global success and impact. Sony's programme of corporate social responsibility in China spans a wide range of social, environmental and commercial factors, and it is important to note that Sony sees CSR in China as a way of enhancing its commercial opportunities, not detracting from them. Key features include:

- Acquiring integrated ISO 14001 certification for all of Sony's eight factories in China

- Collaborating with Chinese research institutions to co-create innovative products and processes, which are both commercially and environmentally sustainable

- Matching aspects of China's culture and its political and institutional environment with Sony's own corporate culture to achieve fit

- Using "green" products made in China to support Sony's commercial and environmental objectives worldwide

6
One step ahead: Tetra Pak

6.1 Introduction

Tetra Pak is the world's leading food processing and packaging company, with activities in more than 150 countries. It employs more than 21,000 staff. Net sales reached €10.9 billion in 2014. Tetra Pak's main products are packages, filling machines, and processing and distribution equipment.

Tetra Pak was founded in Lund, Sweden, in 1951 by Dr Ruben Rausing. His vision was simple: *to make food safe and available, everywhere*. Another of Dr Rausing's founding principles was that a package should save more than it costs, which is aligned with the WWF Climate Savers magnifier approach,[1] that an initiative should "save more emissions than it costs". This principle has been applied to both the commercial and environmental aspects of the company's

---

1   WWF Climate Savers is built on two leadership pillars: 1) Reduction in operational carbon footprint; 2) Magnifiers: company acts as agent of change. For the latter, companies *magnify* their impact by influencing society. There are four basic types of magnifier: 1) Industry sector; 2) Value chain; 3) Public influence; 4) Climate positive approaches. For more details, see http://wwf.panda.org/what_we_do/.

packaging systems. Preventing food losses during product distribution is the key benefit of Tetra Pak cartons, and this reduces both costs and environmental impacts for customers.[2]

While it is easy to think of Tetra Pak as a "beverage carton" company, this underestimates the subtlety of keeping a diverse set of foods safe and available in myriad conditions. Tetra Pak offers 11 basic carton types, each with numerous variations. For example, cartons that keep acidic products – which usually degrade materials rapidly – fresh without preservatives. However, what is good for tomato sauce or wine may not suit a delicate milk product. Likewise, a product designed for a North American distribution system – large trucks covering long distances with pallets stacked high – may not meet the needs of distribution by motorcycle in rural South-East Asia. Constant adaptation is required to ensure that Tetra Pak products continue to meet customer needs.

Tetra Pak has a holistic approach, which addresses environmental impacts at every stage of the life-cycle of their products and services, from design, purchasing of materials, manufacturing, transport, filling and consumption through to the end of the life of the package. The company's aseptic process ensures that both food and packaging materials are free from harmful bacteria when food is packaged. Everything in the production line must be sterile. That includes food and packaging materials, all machinery and the environment in which the packaging takes place. In doing so, Tetra Pak aseptic technology keeps food safe, fresh and flavourful for at least six months – without refrigeration or preservatives. Tetra Pak uses scientifically based life-cycle assessments (LCAs) to analyse the

---

2   Tetra Pak products are known generically as "cartons", and are classed in two types, aseptic cartons and non-aseptic cartons. All products currently made in China are classed as "aseptic cartons". The term "package", used on the previous page, is a unit name.

impact of packaging and processes throughout the whole supply chain.

As a partner in the WWF Climate Savers programme, Tetra Pak has committed to globally reduce its CO_2 emissions while continuing to grow. One ambitious goal was to achieve a 10% reduction of CO_2 emissions compared with 2005, in absolute terms by 2010. This was achieved on time. In its mission statement, Tetra Pak says:

> We believe in responsible industry leadership, creating profitable growth in harmony with environmental sustainability and good corporate citizenship … Our Environmental Policy describes our environmental commitment at every step in the consumption and production chain – from society to raw materials.

So what motivates a multinational company to invest hundreds of millions of euros in China to take the green route? How successful has Tetra Pak been in doing so? What problems and challenges did the company encounter? The case study will attempt to answer some of those questions, looking at various initiatives Tetra Pak has developed.

6.2 Tetra Pak in China

> Thirty years ago when China had just started its economic reform, Tetra Pak came here with a strong belief in the country's market potential. We are grateful for the trust that the Chinese dairy and beverage industry has shown us during this period and for the opportunity of participating in the growth of this industry with our innovative technology and service solutions. Today, China has become one of our largest worldwide markets and will continue to be central to our strategy in the future.
>
> Dennis Jönsson, President and CEO of the Tetra Pak Group

Tetra Pak's presence in China began in 1979 with the introduction of aseptic packaging to its first filling line in the world's most populous country. Interestingly, the name Tetra Pak is rendered in Chinese using two characters as "li le". Literally, "li" can mean "benefit", "interest", "wellness" or "profit", while "le" means "happiness". At the same time, the combination of the two words has another meaning which comes from Buddhism, and means: "being good to the surrounding people, helping them and bringing good to society" (Figure 6.1).

FIGURE 6.1   "Tetra Pak" in Chinese

Thirty years on, Tetra Pak China continues to lead the market despite ever-growing competition from both domestic and international competitors. In 2008, China accounted for nearly 10% of Tetra Pak's global business in terms of revenue. In 2009, the company had 75% of the country's aseptic carton packaging market. Its investment in the country by 2010 had grown to €350 million with a total capacity of approximately 60 billion packs a year in its four Chinese plants, including a new production line added to the Hohhot plant in Inner Mongolia.

> WWF welcomes this agreement between Tetra Pak and the Inner Mongolia Development and Reform Commission. It is another example of the importance of corporate and government collaboration to reduce CO_2 emissions.
>
> Oliver Rapf, WWF International's Head of Business and Industry Engagement on Climate Change, responding to the announcement of the new production line.

According to the Dairy Association of China, the country's dairy industry has grown by 20% over the past decade. Every Chinese person consumes on average 30 kg of dairy products annually, much less than the world average of 120 kg, or average of 300 kg for developed nations. This suggests there is huge growth potential for the dairy industry in China, and this growth in turn will drive the growth of dairy packaging. As Tetra Pak CEO Dennis Jönsson says proudly, "We are growing with China."

6.2.1 Long-term position on sustainability

Tetra Pak believes that environmental protection is an important part of the culture of the company, and regards environmental protection as a priority. As J.T. Luo, Vice President and Cluster Leader of Supply Chain Management for Tetra Pak China, puts it:

> I think this is a very real thing. If any company doesn't look far enough ahead, it can't live for over three years. I've spent 25 years in this company and this company looks very far. If Tetra Pak is going to develop further, it must see further.

Attention to environmental protection on the part of the public can only increase in China, and as one manager puts it, "The one who walks longest will be the one who best protects the environment." To quote J.T. Luo again:

> You cannot only focus on the short-term benefits; you need to look further. If you think it is right, you have to persist and finally there will be a return in the future. In the case of environmental protection, you cannot always look at economic benefits. The benefits may not appear tomorrow, but you should not care too much. This is the only way to walk longer and farther.

6.2.2 Being one step ahead

In 2004 and 2005, when Tetra Pak started to talk about green electricity, recycling and environmental protection with their customers, the response was as if Tetra Pak was talking about something
remote. "They did not know what green energy was," says J.T. Luo,
talking about the attitudes the company encountered initially in
Hohhot. "When we tried to explain to the corporate customers,
they could not accept what we were doing."

But the 2008 Olympics, the milk scandal and the Copenhagen
Conference of 2009 have all led to a change in attitudes. After expe-
riencing the "Green Olympics", interest in environmental protection on the part of both public and the media soared. Tetra Pak felt
that their customers suddenly needed to talk about cooperation on
environmental protection.

6.3 Greening the Chinese supply chain

The convergence of Tetra Pak's corporate values and its mission to
"grow with China" can be seen clearly at the Hohhot plant. Four
concepts and policies are at the heart of the new plant. The first two
– a reliance on green electricity and sustainable sources of paper
pulp – are part of the upstream side of the supply chain. The other
two – reverse logistics or recycling and the decision to become a
leader in sustainable supply chain management (SSCM) – are on
the downstream side. These are not confined to the Hohhot plant,
but are part of Tetra Pak China's overall strategy.

6.3.1 Green electricity

According to J.T. Luo, right at the outset the company set a carbon emission reduction target and invited consultants from Sweden to advise on the green design of the factory and the use of environmentally friendly construction materials:

> The air-conditioning system in the Hohhot plant was planned systematically. The original idea was to improve our energy efficiency. This is a significant problem for the Hohhot plant, because temperatures change greatly within the plant every day. The reason for this is that outdoor temperatures in Hohhot fluctuate very strongly between heat and cold.

It is not uncommon for temperatures in Hohhot to fluctuate by 15 or even 20 degrees between day and night. This is one reason why the plant uses 20 million kilowatts of electricity per year.

The Hohhot facility is the first manufacturing plant in Inner Mongolia, and among the first in China, to establish contracts with government-owned electricity generators to supply exclusively green electricity. In this way the plant aims to reduce its CO_2 emissions by 16,000 tonnes a year, and to encourage investment in clean power generation. It also means that instead of building dedicated power generation for its factory, Tetra Pak is paying a premium to state energy companies so that they will invest in clean generation, and employs third-party auditors to ensure this capacity is provided through the state grid.

The plant has a green space outside with a solar energy system to provide hot water for daily use. All lighting is with low-consumption LED bulbs, and walls are constructed from well-insulated cavity bricks. Thus energy consumption is minimized in a plant that was "built as green".

6.3.2 FSC-certified forests

A key raw material used in packaging is wood pulp. Tetra Pak is working towards accepting wood pulp only from forests certified by the Forest Stewardship Council (FSC). The Yongan Forest in South China was the first forest which Tetra Pak China selected to pass the FSC certification. Tetra Pak doesn't procure any wood products in China because first, the purchasing of wood products is centralized; and second, China is not rich in forest resources. It achieved FSC certification in 2008 after a complex project in which Tetra Pak and the WWF worked with the forest's owner and forestry workers. Carol Yang, Vice President and Cluster Leader of Corporate Communication at Tetra Pak China, explained the background:

> The WWF recommended Yongan Forest. It would have been easier to achieve certification for a northern forest because forests in the north are wholly state-owned. However, forests in south China have complex ownership structures: some are in collective ownership, some in state ownership, some belong to private families and some a combination of the three. In these cases, you have to coordinate all the owners to achieve a satisfactory management level. It took us one year to help Yongan Forestry to pass this certification, a process that included doing research on the local situation and inviting specialists to train the workers. There are many detailed requirements for the FSC certificate, including protecting biodiversity and local people's daily lives, etc. and it takes time to meet all the standards with all the required training.

As awareness of the FSC was relatively low in China, Tetra Pak organized a series of activities to explain what certification meant and the significance of forest protection. Tetra Pak China admitted that this was also a learning process for the company. Kangle Xu, Corporate Communication Executive of Tetra Pak China, said:

> The WWF contributed a lot to this project and invited professors in forestry from the Chinese Academy of Forestry and Renmin University of China to train the forestry managers and workers (at Yongan). WWF devoted great efforts to creating a locally applicable regulation for FSC.

Carol Yang provided more details on the fruitful link with WWF:

> We reached a consensus with WWF in the first place that we both wanted to promote FSC certification in China and help the State Forestry Administration (SFA) and its provincial subsidiaries to do the certification. At this point, it has been clarified that this activity was not linked to our raw material sourcing and our purpose is not necessarily to find forests for future procurement. Our main criterion to consider was around the issue of what are the most sensible and important things we can do in China. Now, Yongan forestry is a benchmark for others.

Tetra Pak's decision to certify Yongan forest in spite of its fragmented ownership structure may be explained as an enactment of its established philosophy of "being one step ahead". The certification initiative is not a one-off: Tetra Pak China is currently helping to certify another forest, Tengchong Forest, following a WWF recommendation. WWF has praised Tetra Pak for its dedicated efforts in advocating and implementing responsible forest management systems in China, an example of the company's dedication to the principle of "protecting what's good".[3] Tetra Pak has already manufactured 1.4 billion FSC-certified packages in China, and the expectation is that eventually all of Tetra Pak's paper packaging will come from forests with FSC certification.

3 Company's motto on the logo.

6.4 Recycling initiatives

What is waste from one process may be raw material for another. As one Tetra Pak manager says, "waste is actually resource placed in the wrong places."

China lacks a well-organized recycling infrastructure, and public awareness of the potential value of recycling is low. Without a large-scale and general interest in recycling, it has been impossible to attract the interest of existing state or private companies. Carol Yang commented: "In the past, our environmental engineers proposed recycling ideas and were refused by those big paper mills, because they were reluctant to introduce a new production line to dispose of the waste packages."

Since 1998, building on experience gained around the world, Tetra Pak China has fostered the growth of small companies specifically fending off the waste from its packaging plants by providing advanced technologies and cooperative manufacturing. By 2010, Tetra Pak was working with more than ten small, privately owned recycling partners. One such business extracts paper pulp from waste cartons in a "washing machine". Another, which Tetra Pak collaboratively developed with a Chinese enterprise in Shandong Province in 2006 and which has been operational since 2008, separates composite materials of aluminium and plastic with a purity of 99.5%.

All these three materials (paper pulp, aluminium and plastic) are in demand as separate commodities. Another approach has been to reuse the combined materials for new products. One process mashes and presses the waste into Caile plate. Benches in Shanghai's Expo Park are now made of this material. A separate business has developed extrusion moulding of the mashed and stirred waste into wood-plastic composite, ideal construction materials for flooring. Concerned about possible environmental risks associated with the production process, Tetra Pak invited Shanghai Environmental Institution to evaluate this technology in the earlier stages of development who subsequently certified that this technology met all the environmental requirements.

In 2009, Tetra Pak China launched a recycling campaign to support the Shanghai World Expo. When the company ran recycling campaigns in the local communities and then donated benches made of Caile plate to the Expo site, it was found that several of Tetra Pak's clients also wanted to participate in these activities. For example, Mengniu and Guangming, two dairy producers, began quickly to manage some waste collection in Shanghai themselves. In the months since the Expo, almost all Tetra Pak clients have inquired if Tetra Pak could make a presentation on environmental protection and give them some ideas for their own waste recycling. Meanwhile the demand for products of both reprocessing technologies is growing, specifically for outdoor furniture and dustbins.

6.5 Becoming a dairy supply chain leader in sustainability

In the Chinese market, Tetra Pak straddles two industries. Although primarily a packaging company, its operations are entirely tied up with the dairy industry. Thus both supply chains are crucial to its business.

Tetra Pak China's dependence on the dairy industry was brought sharply into focus by the adulterated milk scandal of 2008. This crisis caused widespread distrust of all domestic dairy brands including Mengniu and Yili. Facing rapidly growing demand for dairy products in China, some dairy farmers adulterated the raw milk with melamine in order to boost protein levels, and hence prices.[4] This practice had apparently been widespread among dairy farmers for some time, in spite of the toxic effects on humans, especially when the milk was used in infant formula. In autumn 2008 six infants died from kidney damage, and more than 800 were hospitalized. It is estimated that adulterated milk products affected over 300,000 people. Consequently customers switched to more expensive but trusted international brands.

Tetra Pak China was affected too. The expected growth rate for 2008 was 16%, but Tetra Pak China achieved only 5% growth that year. This is a textbook example of supply chain disruption; the disruption of one material, raw milk, causes disruption of the whole chain.

Tetra Pak is neither a dairy producer nor a pasture-land owner, so the company is able to grow only so long as this industry itself is developing sustainably. In a long-term project to reform the dairy industry, Tetra Pak has for more than ten years sponsored a cooperative research programme with the School of Economics of Renmin University in Beijing. The two institutions are trying to transform a private and fragmented dairy farm model into an intensive and modern one.

Yun Jiang, Climate Savers Senior Programme Officer at WWF China, said:

> Tetra Pak is a good example of how promoting good ideas can affect supply chains in China. Tetra Pak is doing a good job in coping with climate change and its actions are having great influence over dairy enterprises. For example, Tetra Pak China encouraged Mengniu to join the Climate Savers project.

4   Melamine contains 66% nitrogen but is toxic to humans. The State and Provincial Food and Drug Administration uses the level of nitrogen as an indicator of protein level, which is difficult to measure directly.

Alongside its packaging technology, Tetra Pak has introduced new low-energy production lines to benefit its customers, such as a milk-separating centrifuge that saved 30% of milk production costs. It was through this introduction that Tetra Pak China helped its customer, Mengniu, to learn about the Climate Savers programme run by the WWF. Mengniu is now in the process of applying for Climate Savers membership.

Tetra Pak is also managing the certification of pasture-lands. State-owned pasture-lands possess modern equipment and good-quality cows, but are weak in management. Tetra Pak has set up a professional team to upgrade Chinese pasture-lands by offering management training and guidelines, helping them to be more efficient and reduce CO_2 emissions. More than 30 pasture-lands have now achieved EU standards. Tetra Pak opened a training school for private dairy farmers, teaching them modern ways of raising dairy cows. The company also produced a series of educational films and wrote books in partnership with CCTV 7 (China Central Television Channel 7) and distributed them for free. Later, when some pirated DVDs of these films were found in markets, Tetra Pak China was delighted: the piracy shows that many people are eager to learn from the materials they produced!

6.6 The Hohhot plant

On 8 July 2009, Tetra Pak opened a new plant for the manufacture of packaging for dairy products in Hohhot, Northern China. The company invested €60 million in the plant, which has a production capacity of 11 billion packs a year. This is Tetra Pak's fourth plant in China, and it represents an ambitious scaling up of production as the company seeks to keep pace with the soaring demand for aseptic packaging in China. Even as the plant opened, Tetra Pak announced that it was investing a further €53 million to set up an additional production line that would increase production by 10 billion packs, bringing its total capacity in China to 60 billion packs.

The challenges in designing and building the plant were immense. Hohhot is the capital of the Inner Mongolian Autonomous Region, a remote northern region where supply and logistics are, to say the least, problematic. The site was chosen so that the plant would be close to key customers: Mengniu and Yili, two of China's leading dairy producers, are both based in Hohhot. This positioning gives Tetra Pak a strong strategic advantage.

The Hohhot plant has a number of features that mark it out. First, there is its size. The expansion to 20 billion packs a year in 2010 made it the largest Tetra Pak factory in China. It is also one of the largest industrial complexes in Inner Mongolia and represents a major investment in the region. Second, there is the plant's green design. Perhaps surprisingly, given the logistical challenges, Tetra Pak decided to manage both of its main inputs – electricity and paper pulp – in a sustainable way. Tetra Pak has set itself the mission of greening the entire dairy value chain in China.

6.7 Enablers of implementation

A number of factors at Tetra Pak have enabled the implementation of these innovative solutions in China. These include:

- Long-term position on sustainability

- Being "one step ahead"

- Clear sustainable strategy and business model

- Senior management support

- Congruence of economic and sustainable benefits
- Environment-related key performance indicators (KPIs)
- Supportive organizational structure

6.7.1 Clear sustainable strategy and business model

Tetra Pak's policy on responsible business is expressed as 4Rs: renewing, reducing, recycling and responsibility, a life-cycle assessment (LCA) and holistic approach towards sustainability. Initially, this policy was passed down from company headquarters. However, Tetra Pak came to understand that the Chinese market was different, and there is local adaptation of the 4Rs. This is shown in Tetra Pak China's focus on recycling. Carol Yang said:

> Basically we follow the global strategy. However, there are some issues in China's market, e.g. 1) the concept of LCA is still novel to most people; 2) there is a limited base of people with LCA knowledge constraining our ability to implement LCA. In fact, we do conduct LCA studies in our four factories in China, but do not feel the need to communicate the concept yet. The pressing environmental issue in China is recycling and that's where our focus is for now and the near future. As one can imagine, with the market size, China could be dragging down the global recycling rate if we do not put enough emphasis on it.

6.7.2 Senior management support

Tetra Pak's CEO, Dennis Jönsson, comes to China every year to meet key account customers and show support for sustainable initiatives in China. As Carol Yang said:

> China is the largest market for Tetra Pak. Only when we do well in China can we succeed globally. Otherwise, China will become the largest burden. Therefore, Tetra Pak headquarters has given us significant support. Our factory in Hohhot is

designed to use green power, which received significant support from headquarters. Hohhot is one of Tetra Pak's largest factories. One hundred per cent green electricity in such a big factory has played an important role in reducing our global carbon footprint.

As Carol Yang says:

In a sense, FSC certification may be regarded as a charitable activity. But if the charitable things you do are not related to the whole business, it is difficult to be sustainable: on the contrary, I think if the things you do can both benefit society and long-term enterprise development, such charity will be sustainable, because it is a win–win situation.

6.7.3 Environment-related key performance indicators (KPIs)

According to Kangle Xu and J.T. Luo, environmental measures are built into Tetra Pak's performance measurement system. Everyone is measured against environmental KPIs. Kangle Xu claimed that "in fact, for Tetra Pak, no particularly large organizational changes are needed when conducting environmental protection. We've been doing this for a long time and this is the company's culture. So, everyone's job is associated with this."

6.7.4 Supportive organizational structure

Tetra Pak global has a special team called the Global Environmental Protection team, and this is mirrored in similar structures at country level. These local teams report to the global environmental protection team as well as to the corporate communications department. This shows the company pays much attention to environmental protection, and the dual reporting system ensures the local policy is aligned with that from HQ.

6.8 Problems and challenges

At the same time, there have been considerable barriers to the implementation of Tetra Pak's ideas and programmes. Some are intrinsic to China's economy at its current stage of development, others are down to Tetra Pak itself. These include:

- Lack of awareness and environmental education among the public

- Lack of a waste classification system in China

- Lack of proper promotion prevents innovation dissemination

- Lack of coordination among sustainable initiatives in Tetra Pak China

6.8.1 Lack of awareness and environmental education among the public

As noted above, awareness is now increasing. For example, FSC certification is required by many export customers such as IKEA, and Tetra Pak encourages their suppliers to meet standards required by the European market. But these are new concepts for the public in China, and this has created some friction. Carol Yang said:

> It is unfair that people challenge us on our 10% CO_2 reduction. Actually, it is a big step forward because there is no support from the government and no system of garbage classification. It is frustrating that the government and the media do not consider our work with an objective and reasonable attitude. We have spent RMB 150 million in the past decade (in doing this), and few other enterprises could afford this project.

Kangle Xu also commented:

Sometimes the public will misunderstand our work. There is a Chinese saying that goes "the more work you do, the more mistakes you will make". Tetra Pak is one of the first enterprises to conduct environmental projects in China, but other companies do not pay much attention to our achievements; rather, they criticize that we have not been doing enough. In addition, they think that our work must be motivated by a hidden agenda, our production will cause endless troubles, or we are only motivated to make more money. They don't believe that enterprises are willing to pay back to society. We face great pressure based on this misunderstanding but it is hard to explain it to the public. It discouraged us in our work to some extent.

6.8.2 Lack of waste classification system in China

A weak garbage classification system has prevented Tetra Pak from employing advanced technologies such as waste incineration. This is important, as incinerating unclassified garbage will produce more CO_2 as a result. This is not just a matter of technology: China has modern incinerators, but not the systems to make best use of them. In countries that expect households to sort their garbage everyone participates in the system, thus higher standards can be expected from business. Such a system still needs to be introduced in China. The lack of coordination between different departments and between central and local governments also makes it very hard to develop new practices.

6.8.3 Lack of coordination among sustainable initiatives in Tetra Pak China

At Tetra Pak, capacity building includes four solutions to achieve a 10% reduction in CO_2 emissions. The first is to employ green electricity. The second is to continuously improve technology to reduce energy consumption. The third is to help clients reduce the cost of their packaging and increase production efficiency. The fourth refers to the recycling of waste materials. However, there is no single team that completely controls these four solutions, which are operated by four departments. For example, recycling is the responsibility of the department of environmental protection; supply chain looks after green electricity; and the department of operations works with clients on innovation. One manager suggested that it could be improved if the four solutions could be coordinated across the departments.

6.9 The final word

Despite the issues outlined above and other problems, Tetra Pak has been a successful innovator in terms of its supply chain relationships with both suppliers and customers, and both have seen benefits as a result. It is hoped that over time, these benefits will be felt more widely in China; and, of course, by Tetra Pak itself. Kangle Xu said:

> In the past, enterprises tended to conduct business secretly, which will lead to one of two end-points: indulging in empty talk, or no proper promotion of work that is done. Tetra Pak is not an enterprise working mainly on environmental technology. However, we are doing a good job, and so some other enterprises are willing to follow us.
>
> We believe in responsible industry leadership, creating profitable growth in harmony with environmental sustainability and good corporate citizenship.
>
> Tetra Pak Social Responsibility Report

6.10 Case summary

Tetra Pak, the world's leading food packaging company, has a long tradition of commitment to environmental and social sustainability. In China, Tetra Pak has created a sustainable supply chain by directly greening its upstream and downstream supply chains. Key areas of focus have been forestry certification, pasture-land management and investing in and developing recycling equipment and systems. During this initiative Tetra Pak has partnered a wide variety of stakeholders including farmers, wholesalers, government departments and agencies, universities, NGOs and even garbage collectors. Key features include:

- Working with the downstream supply chain to improve rates of recycling of used packaging

- Establishing a carton collection system in China, where waste categories are poorly defined

- Working with waste collectors and recycling companies to collect and recycle thrown-away milk cartons

- Engaging with local authorities to get access to communities and develop industry standards

- Initiating and providing financial support to the China Packaging Association, which drafted the first circular economy law in China

- In recycling, identifying where Tetra Pak's support can be most useful in areas such as technology development, growing the recycling infrastructure and increasing consumer awareness, and then working with local partners to push each of these areas forward

7
Sustainable supply chain strategy: Vanke

7.1 Introduction

Established as a small trading company in 1984, Vanke has become the world's largest residential real estate developer in terms of sales revenue. In 1991 it became the second listed company on the Shenzhen Stock Exchange (SZSE). In 2010, Vanke was the first Chinese residential company to achieve sales revenue of more than RMB 100 billion, and in 2012 it became the first real estate company in the world to achieve sales revenue of more than US$20 billion. In 2013, it had sold floor space of 14.90 million m^2 with a sales revenue of RMB 170.94 billion, an industry record. Within a highly fragmented industry in China, Vanke had a market share of 2.09% in 2013. In 2014, it had sold floor space of 18.06 million m^2 with a sales revenue of RMB 215.13 billion and again renewed the industry record (see Figure 7.1).

Headquartered in Shenzhen, Vanke's business covers more than 60 cities in mainland China. In 2014 Vanke had four regional headquarters: Beijing headquarters for the Bohai Economic Rim with

FIGURE 7.1   Vanke last ten years sales by floor space and sales revenue

Source: Vanke annual report 2014.

11 subsidiaries, Shanghai headquarters for the Yangtze River Delta region with 13 subsidiaries, Guangzhou-Shenzhen headquarters for the Pearl River Delta region with 11 subsidiaries and Chengdu headquarters for central and western parts of China with eight subsidiaries. In 2013, the Guangzhou-Shenzhen region contributed 31% of the annual sales revenue, with Shanghai and Beijing contributing 27% each and the Chengdu region contributing 16% (see Table 7.1).

In addition, Vanke started its international journey in 2013 by cooperating with leading local developers to enter markets in Hong Kong, the United States and Singapore. Together with the New World Development Company, Vanke won a bid for a major residential project on top of a newly constructed railway station in Hong Kong. It also formed a joint venture with New York-based Tishman Speyer Properties to develop two luxury condominiums in San Francisco. In another joint venture, with Keppel Land Limited, Vanke took a 30% stake in a condominium project.

Regions	2013 sales revenue (RMB 1 billion)	2013 sales revenue by percentage	Coverage
Guangzhou-Shenzhen 18)	52.39	31%	Shenzhen, Huizhou, Guangzhou, Qingyuan, Foshan, Dongguan, Zhuhai, Zhongshan, Xiamen, Changsha, Fuzhou, Haikou, Sanya, Putian, Nanning, Quanzhou, Zhangzhou, Shishi
Beijing (20)	45.4	27%	Beijing, Langfang, Tangshan, Qinhuangdao, Tianjin, Shenyang, Anshan, Fushun, Qingdao, Changchun, Jilin, Dalian, Yantai, Taiyuan, Jinzhong, Yingkou, Jinan, Jimo, Jinan, Pingdu
Shanghai (18)	46.05	27%	Shanghai, Nantong, Jiaxing, Hangzhou, Wenzhou, Suzhou, Wuxi, Nanjing, Zhenjiang, Yangzhou, Ningbo, Nanchang, Hefei, Wuhu, Xuzhou, Changzhou, Kunshan, Fuyang
Chengdu (9)	27.1	16%	Chengdu, Wuhan, Chongqing, Xi'an, Kunming, Guiyang, Urumchi, Nanchong, Zhengzhou
Total	170.94	100%	61 cities in mainland China as at end of 2013

TABLE 7.1 Vanke regional sales revenue and geographic coverage

Source: Vanke annual report, 2014.

During its first two decades (1984–2004), under the founder and Chairman Wang Shi's leadership, Vanke was transformed from a diversified conglomerate to a specialized real estate and property management company. Established originally as a trading company, Vanke first engaged in the corn trading business and then moved to trading "whatever was profitable", including textiles, electronics, chemicals and medical devices. In the late 1980s Vanke diversified further into areas such as printing, jewellery, manufacturing, department stores, and even film production and electric power distribution. After 2000, Vanke decided to concentrate on real estate.

In 2001, a research project undertaken by the company convinced Wang Shi that China's residential housing market would be big enough to support the company's organic growth. Vanke started positioning itself as a mainstream residential developer, focusing on building quality homes for middle-class people to live in (rather than the high-end or property investment market). Vanke adhered to the principle of "holding no land, putting off no home sales, and refraining from bidding for highly priced land", in an era when buying and then selling land for a higher price without actually building on it was popular. Vanke also aimed to achieve a fair and fast return on its investments. In 2013, 91.5% of the residential houses it sold were smaller than 144 m^2 (1,550 square feet), suitable for middle-class families. Sixty per cent of new homes coming to market were sold within one month.

Between 2004 and 2014, Vanke focused further still on residential property development, gaining a cumulative competitive edge in the housing industry. The Vanke brand became the first well-known trademark in the industry in China. Vanke was the first to introduce property management services to China, and its property management division is among the first ISO 9002 certified property service providers in the country. The Vanke Property Customers Club is also the first customer (property owner) relations organization in

China's housing industry. Finally, Vanke was the first real estate enterprise in China to hire a third-party institution to carry out an all-round customer satisfaction survey every year.

Vanke realizes that the housing industry consumes a high level of resources, both during the building process – which consumes large amounts of steel, concrete and logistics resources – and after: houses, once they become residences, consume energy, water and other resources. Vanke is dedicated to leading the industry in energy conservation and emission reduction, and also promotes green buildings and housing industrialization.[1]

As it is a leader in the industry, Vanke believes it should also be more sustainable than other companies. In promoting its green vision, however, Vanke faces a number of challenges. How can Vanke balance costs with its mission to provide affordable apartments for ordinary people? How can it maintain high-quality standards and meet customer expectations while providing more complex services? Should Vanke still focus on residential buildings, or should it diversify? After describing the background of Wang Shi and China's property development supply chain management, this case study looks at Vanke's internal sustainability initiatives, its initiatives with suppliers and customers, and its future plans.

---

1   Housing industrialization is the integration of production, supply, sale and service by linking housing design, manufacture, assembly, construction and management together. It has several purposes: increasing labour productivity, replacing expensive manual labour with machines, accelerating the pace of construction, putting new projects into operation more quickly, reducing costs and improving quality. It includes the extensive use of prefabricated factory-finished large-sized elements and the conversion of production into a mechanized and continuously flowing process of assembly and installation of buildings and structure made from prefabricated assemblies and parts. (see http://blueislandmauritius.com/housing-industrialisation/).

7.2 Wang Shi's vision and beliefs

Since founding and leading Vanke in 1984, Wang Shi has profoundly shaped its corporate visions, ethics and management strategies. In recent years he has led environmental initiatives among Chinese private sector companies, particularly in natural habitat preservation, garbage recycling and forest conservation. Internationally, he sits on the board of WWF in the US and is a council member of the World Economic Forum Global Agenda Council on Governance for Sustainability. Wang Shi's beliefs are woven into Vanke's corporate culture. "Architecture – Our Tribute to Life" is the core ideology of Vanke. This ideology shows respect for nature and society, and demands that Vanke should respond actively to environmental challenges by minimizing its environmental impact in terms of both construction and future home use. Vanke also believes that residential architecture is intertwined with life in every aspect. As a home builder, Vanke has a high regard for people, and sees its mission as providing them safe and peaceful green homes while creating a harmonized and healthy living environment.

7.3 Vanke in China

The residential property development process in China generally includes five steps: acquisition of land, project design, project construction, project sales and property management. A divergent developer supply chain links all these processes and involves upstream and downstream supply chain partners (see Figure 7.2). In the first step, developer companies make investment decisions based on feasibility analysis. Developers then purchase land from local government or from other land providers with loans from financial

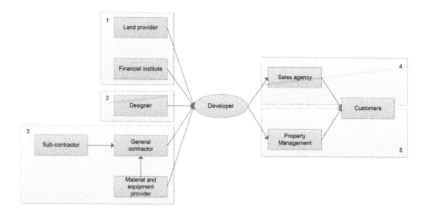

FIGURE 7.2   Real estate developers' supply chain management in China

institutions. In the second step, developers may involve external design companies for project planning and design. In the construction process, developers send invitations to general contractors for bidding; the selected general contractor may bring along its own subcontractors for construction. Material and equipment providers may supply the developer or the general contractor directly. During the construction process, developers outsource project sales to professional sales agencies. Property management companies are involved in the final process of providing after-sale services.

This case study focuses mainly on the third and fifth processes, which involve Vanke suppliers and customers. In 2013, Vanke publicly announced its seven types of supplier (general contractor, construction supervision, decoration general contractor, doors and windows, landscape, foundation engineering, material and equipment), totalling 824 qualified suppliers. Vanke suppliers were classified into four levels according to criticality and quality performance: A, B, C and D. D suppliers are those that should be phased out; C suppliers are adequate but not suitable for developing long-term relationships. B suppliers are key suppliers and can be developed into strategic suppliers, and A suppliers are critical suppliers to which the company should stay close and develop good relationships. There were 35 A suppliers on the list.

7.4 Vanke internal sustainability initiatives

Vanke's internal sustainability initiatives focus on three aspects: fully finished units, prefabrication (prefab) and green building. Wang Shi says:

> Frankly, Vanke's initial promotion of housing industrialization is to enhance its competitiveness, not for environmental protection, but later we found that it can save energy and material, which is consistent with the requirements of the green economy: we started promoting green building in a conscious way.

7.4.1 Fully finished units

Contrary to the Western practice of providing fully finished property, Chinese real estate developers tended, between the 1980s and 2000s, to provide rough apartments. The buyers of these new properties had to decorate throughout. Housing decoration is always a heavy commitment in terms of investment and time for Chinese buyers, especially for buyers who purchase their first property, because the whole process normally takes more than a month, and buyers need to deal with various different kinds of construction service provider.

Fully finished units have several advantages, including more price bargaining power, better quality control, less waste created during the decoration process and less disturbance for neighbours. Companies can buy materials more cheaply than individual buyers, and their greater knowledge of materials allows better quality control. It was estimated that providing fully finished units would reduce the waste generated during decoration by two tons per household. Companies that do their own decoration also reduce the disturbance and noise caused during the process.

Delivering fully finished units is now common practice in the industry. Vanke was among the first major developers to adopt this method. In 2012, Vanke delivered more than 80% of its houses fully finished; in 2013, this rose to more than 90%. At the end of 2013, in total Vanke delivered 99,500 fully finished units.

7.4.2 Prefabs

As Vanke grew rapidly, its construction site management became more and more complex. Inspired by the experience of the Japanese construction industry, Wang Shi believed prefab construction offered a solution. Soaring labour costs made prefab even more necessary.

Initially, prefabrication was adopted in Japan as a way to improve and control quality for high-rise buildings. Some of the construction components are precast at the factory and then transported and assembled at the construction site. Prefab components normally include exterior walls, stairs, beams, balconies and floors. Prefab allows for greater standardization, more precision and faster construction cycles. It also offers opportunities to reduce energy, water, waste and material use, all of which are in line with Vanke's green strategy.

Vanke set up its Architecture Research Centre (ARC) in Dongguan, Guangdong Province, in 1999 as a base for prefab research. This is now the largest R&D facility in the Chinese construction industry. In 2007 the Vanke ARC was approved as the national base for housing industrialization by the Ministry of Housing and

Urban-Rural Development (MOHURD). In an internal study by ARC the prefab method, compared with the traditional method, was found to reduce energy consumption by 20%, water consumption by 63%, timber formwork consumption by 87% and waste production by 91% per m².

In 2010, 1.06 million m² of prefabs were built; the number increased to 2.72 million m² in 2011, and remained at that level in 2012. Some of the new prefab applications use steel or aluminium rather than wood moulding, which reduces wood consumption and protects the environment while at the same time avoiding quality problems such as surface cracks and hollowing.

Vanke sets annual targets for prefabricated concrete, pre-assembled inner walls and plaster-free inner and outer walls. In 2013 the applications for these three were 8.3%, 38.8% and 29.1% respectively. In 2014 the ratios were 27%, 100% and 87% respectively which all surpassed the targets of 20%, 60% and 50% set at the beginning of the year. Vanke believes that while fully finished units may be easy for competitors to imitate, prefabs are much more difficult to copy as accumulated industry knowledge is required. Having worked with prefabs for nearly 15 years, Vanke has a potential first-mover advantage.

7.4.3 Green building

MOHURD developed a Green Building Rating System (known as "the Three Star System" which is comparable to the LEED system, with three stars the highest standard) in 2006–2007. This aims to reduce China's CO_2 intensity (CO_2 per unit of GDP) by 40–50% by 2020. The system, which is voluntary, covers key aspects of the construction process such as land, energy, water and material use, as well as indoor and outdoor environmental quality and property management. Stars were given based on how many criteria been met. It believed that buildings will be required to meet at least a one-star standard in the future.

To promote its green vision and make houses affordable to customers, Vanke focuses on low-cost green technologies such as natural light, exterior insulation, water conservation and ventilation methods that leverage natural elements (such as new types of wind chimney to enhance ventilation) as well as waste-reduction technologies such as sorting, recycling and composting machines.

In 2009, Vanke built China's first three-star project, Shenzhen Vanke City Phase IV, the only three-star green building finished in that year. In 2010, Vanke built 0.75 million m^2 of three-star green buildings, accounting for 54% of the total built nationwide. In that year its new headquarters, the Vanke Centre, was recognized as China's first LEED-certified platinum office building. In 2011 Vanke created 2.68 million m^2 of three-star green housing, accounting for 50.7% of the national total. Vanke is building a second research centre in Beijing with the collaboration of UK consultancy BRE (Building Research Establishment), to explore low-cost environmental technologies for use in multi-storey buildings. In 2012, in a fluctuating market, 1.22 million m^2 of three-star green housing was built, accounting for 44% of building nationwide; in 2013, the total was 1.41 million m^2 or 34% of building nationwide; in 2014, 1.64 million m^2 of three-star green housing had been built.

7.4.4 Social sustainability: affordable housing

Vanke has always focused on giving full play to its advantages in the field of real estate and fulfilling its social responsibility. To support government policy, it has actively participated in the building of affordable housing since 2006. In 2007, the Commune project, backed by Vanke, was completed in Guangzhou. This was the first low-rent housing project sponsored by an enterprise to address the housing needs of low-income people; traditionally, provision of low-income housing has been the responsibility of government. The Commune is also listed as a pilot low-rent housing project for low-income people by the Housing and Urban-Rural Development Department of Guangdong Province. By the end of 2013 Vanke had built a total of 5.47 million m² of affordable housing. Calculated by the national standard of 13 m² per person, it was estimated that 420,000 people had benefited from this.

7.4.5 Continuous learning from other leading companies

Vanke is dedicated to learning and has always looked for benchmark companies to learn from. Vanke first learned the concept of after-sale services from Sony about three decades ago, at a time when not many business people in China were familiar with the term, to say nothing of ordinary customers. Every property was leased from the state, and no one thought about what would happen after the properties were sold. At that time Vanke was a distributor for Sony which, unlike traditional Chinese companies, not only provided high-quality products but also provided equally high-quality after-sale services. Inspired by Sony, Vanke later became the first real estate company to introduce property management into China.

Vanke also learned from Sun Hung Kai Properties (SHKP), its first role model in the real estate industry. SHKP was founded in 1963 and was listed on the Hong Kong Stock Exchange in 1972. It is one of the largest property companies in Hong Kong and specializes in premium-quality residential and commercial projects for sale and investment. Vanke learned its real estate development process, customer relationship management and the concept of quality management from SHKP. Following SHKP's example, Vanke set up Vanke Customer Clubs to maintain customer relationships and provide value-added services. A Vanke Customer Club was set up in each city where Vanke operates, and is normally divided into three levels by bonus points: blue card membership, gold card membership and platinum card membership. Each membership enjoys corresponding benefits such as promotional information, bonus gifts, and discounts in Vanke partner stores for card members and their direct relatives when purchasing Vanke property.

Vanke also learned from another real estate benchmark, the US company Pulte Homes. Mainly through analysis of publicly available information, Vanke found it has a similar business model, scale and development pattern as Pulte, which also operates in various geographic areas (it has residential developments in more than 20 states in the USA). Pulte had remained profitable for more than 50 years with an average return on equity of above 16%. Vanke learned Pulte's recipes for success including outstanding customer service (lifetime service), customer segmentation and branding. Based on Pulte customer service steps, Vanke invented its own customer service methodology, which it calls the "6+2 method". This method summarizes the six main interfaces between Vanke and customers and two long-term methods. The six interfaces are: review houses, sign contract, wait for completion, house inspection, move and settle down. Vanke designed corresponding services for each step to solve problems and concerns for customers. The two long-term methods are life-cycle management and continuous care, which reflect Vanke's life-cycle management for owner properties and the whole community.

Lastly, Vanke learned from several Japanese companies such as Toyota Housing and Taisei Corporation. Wang Shi strongly believes that Vanke's future lies in the industrialization of residential development. He believes in "building houses in the way cars are manufactured". In 2006, Vanke hired a senior R&D expert from Toyota Housing who was responsible for its industrialization research. In 2012 Vanke started its "Qian Yi Plan" (千亿计划:

"Qian" means "one thousand", "Yi" means "one hundred million RMB"), to invest RMB 100 million and send 1,000 engineers to study at Japanese construction sites. Vanke had cooperated with Taisei Corporation on a project in 2005, knowing that it has a specialized concrete prefab subsidiary. During collaboration Taisei gave Vanke considerable access to its construction sites, and has become its most important learning base.

7.5 Sustainable initiatives with suppliers

7.5.1 Requirements for suppliers

Once Vanke acquires land, a team of architects, engineers and planners designs the projects and sets materials procurement, energy efficiency and other standards in order to contract builders and other suppliers to construct the project. Normally the tender is open to the three or four most qualified vendors based on the company's centralized database of more than 4,000 companies. The selected vendors are required to sign a contract agreeing to follow China's labour laws on worker pay and safety, insurance for work-related injuries, breaks during hot weather and so on. If they are found to be breaking the law, vendors can be fined or lose their status as a Vanke vendor.

Contracts also include Vanke's own requirements (known as the "Sunshine Agreement" within Vanke) prohibiting bribery, such as giving project-related gifts to Vanke officials or funding banquets for Vanke personnel. For quality issues, suppliers may be given a yellow or red card by Vanke, which means a suspension of relationships for half a year and one year respectively. A commercial bribe could place a company on Vanke's blacklist, which means the relationship is terminated permanently. Vanke is famous within the industry for not bribing government officials in order to get land, a principle set by Wang Shi and followed closely by the whole company.

Additional protection for vendors' workers is also provided by Vanke. Non-payment or underpayment of workers is not an infrequent practice in the construction industry. Vanke withholds a portion of the contract price until the project is complete and workers have been paid in full. In the case of a contractor failing or delaying payment, Vanke will pay the workers directly from the fund. Vanke also requires contractors to provide workers with air-conditioned accommodation in Southern China where the temperature during the summer is very high, clean drinking water (normally one cannot drink directly from a tap in China), Internet access and so on. By making sure these measures are in place, Vanke shows respect for workers and also demonstrates its belief that product quality is directly linked to workers' satisfaction.

7.5.2 Collaboration with suppliers

Every day hundreds of thousands of people are working hard on construction sites for projects developed by Vanke. Illness caused by poverty has brought about many problems for workers and their families. Vanke is always concerned about these problems. In April 2011, Vanke announced that RMB 5 million would be invested from its Corporate Citizenship Fund to initiate the "Spring Action" project. The project aims to help workers who cannot afford the high treatment cost of serious illnesses, their own or those of their families. In addition, Vanke works together with contractors and other partners to establish a mechanism for workers to help each other.

In 2012 Vanke and WWF reached an agreement on environmental protection and green sustainable development for 2012–16. One area of cooperation focused on the GFTN (Global Forest and Trade Network), aiming to leverage Vanke's influence on its supply chain to reduce the consumption of timber, protect the rainforest and combat climate change. Wang Shi says:

> Vanke is impressed by WWF's environmental goal to achieve zero net deforestation and degradation by 2020, and the vision to have 100% renewable energy supply by 2050. I hope that through the partnership, Vanke can do our fair share to conserve the planet, through jointly defined targets on carbon reduction, eco-management and forest preservation. The international technical support of WWF will keep us on the right track to hit those targets.

On 9 May 2013, GFTN, Vanke Purchasing and the Vanke Corporate Citizen Office held a joint training and communication session for all four of its wood flooring suppliers, all of which were among the top ten flooring companies in China in terms of sales revenue. The meeting finalized the timetable for sustainable wood supply chain management and the action plan for 2013. Bing Shen, Head of the President's Office at Vanke, says:

> Three years ago, 90% of our wood flooring source was unknown, but today 84% has been certified by international organizations, and we can trace the remaining 16% to its original place. Vanke has reduced its wood flooring suppliers from nine to four. In the process, Vanke introduced GFTN certification to all its suppliers, and five of them were eventually certified. We place more orders with those who are willing to cooperate with us on this.

Vanke further committed to having at least 12 suppliers adopt GB/T23331 Energy Management Standards (comparable to ISO 50001), and having more than 90% of its centralized purchasing suppliers achieve the ISO 9001 Quality Management Certificate and ISO 14001 Environmental Management Certificate by the end of 2018. Beyond these commitments Vanke also plans to develop carbon calculation tools for residents and promote low-carbon lifestyles.

7.5.3 Learning with suppliers

Vanke holds an annual conference with all its suppliers, during which Vanke informs suppliers of its focus for the coming year. Excellent suppliers are rewarded, best practices are shared, and company and suppliers have dinner together. For A and B suppliers, Vanke requires the purchasing team to conduct formal meetings with them on a half-yearly basis. Attendees review the current status of projects, report quality assessment results, discuss questions and transfer new quality values. Jun Du, General Manager of the Procurement Management Department and Customer Relationship Management, tells one story about sharing best practices:

> Once we found one of our flooring suppliers was very good at contract management. They set up a file for every contract, from when the contract was signed, when they purchased the raw material, test results, photos of the manufacturing process, the test results of the final goods, to the quality of the final product. They kept all the records, one contract and one set of records, which makes it very transparent ... we asked all of our material suppliers to learn from it.

Demonstration meetings are also held for contractors, usually at construction sites: "we invited our contractors and subsidiary companies' managers, on-site, to learn the best practice and what is Vanke's quality value and construction site management".

7.6 Sustainable initiatives with customers

7.6.1 Care for customers

In 2000, Vanke became the first Chinese property company to invite a third party to conduct a survey on customer satisfaction. In 2012, Vanke added one additional question in the survey questionnaire:

"How many friends do you have in your community?" Vanke President Liang Yu comments:

> Care for each other in the community is a symbol of harmony ... we found that each householder has on average 12 friends ... If that number in your community is below 12, the level of satisfaction drops significantly. We therefore require the property service teams to organize events to promote more contacts and communication between property owners ... the survey results are directly linked to their bonuses.

Vanke organizes social events such as parties, concerts and sports outings in order to foster stronger community bonding. For instance, in September 2014 Vanke held a "Happy Family Festival" that has been running for 12 years. In 2014 the festival covered 56 cities, approximately 101,000 families and 258,000 people. Through watching live programmes and playing games, community members are provided with a friendly and happy environment in which to communicate. At this year's event, Vanke also promoted "neighbourhood conventions" in various communities. Neighbourhood conventions are normally created by the communities over several rounds of discussion, summary and announcement, and once confirmed require all community members to obey the rules of the convention. The first neighbourhood convention was started in Liangzhu New Town, a cultural heritage site near Hangzhou. The story of Liangzhu is told in more detail below.

Vanke also focused on service innovations that were driven by customer demands. In 2012, Vanke began to provide "the fifth canteen", "multi-storage" and "happy relay" services to cover customer needs in catering, storage and convenience (e.g. receive parcels, housekeeping) in some pilot cities. In 2013, to cater for the increasing demand for online shopping needs, Vanke and its partners launched various projects including the "Vanke-Yunda nationwide parcel partnership", "Vanke-Tmall self-pick service partnership" and "Unicome database system", which provide convenient services for customers to send and collect parcels. The mobile application (app) "Living Here" was developed for Vanke customers, and "Happy to Help" was developed for property service staff, both of which could be used on smartphones. A customer service management system and call centres were also launched.

7.6.2 Transformation from real estate developer to "urban-supporting service provider": Liangzhu New Town

In 2012, a WeChat (a mobile text and voice messaging communication application) article "A magic town in China – Liangzhu New Town", spread quickly among the app's users, with more than 30 million people reading it. What happened to the town and why was its popularity so great?

Liangzhu New Town is considered an exemplar of a new rural lifestyle in China under the backdrop of China's mega scale urbanization and also represents Vanke's new business model: being an urban-supporting service provider.

Liangzhu New Town is located 16 km to the north-west of Hangzhou City, Zhejiang Province, and 2 km from the Liangzhu heritage site, which has a history of 5,000 years extending back to the New Stone Age. A large number of exquisite jade artefacts were excavated at the sites, which are believed to have been created by ancient civilizations. Facing a river and with hills at the back, from a *feng shui* perspective the geographic location of Liangzhu New Town is considered very suitable for people to live.

In 2000 the second-largest local developer, Nandu, signed a joint development agreement with the local government for the Liangzhu New Town project. The project covers a total area of about 667 hectares, with half consisting of natural views of mountains and the river, and the other half for development, with an estimated household capacity of 15,000 and a total capacity of 30,000 to 50,000 people, the size of a small town in Europe. Nandu planned to develop the area as "a model for Chinese living" that could have an impact on the world. It invited international architect David Chipperfield to design the Liangzhu Museum, and spent more than RMB 30 million on construction. In 2006 Nandu shifted its corporate strategy from real estate to finance and Vanke took over the project. It was the largest single project carried out by the Vanke Group.

As well as residential development, Vanke responded to owners' needs by building various public facilities such as a museum, hotels, a church, schools, a waste classification promotion and education centre, community cafeteria, a community farm and courier services – even though these were normally the responsibility of government. Vanke involved famous design companies for these public facilities, including the Tsushima Design Studio which designed the Meilizhou Church, and Zhejing University School of Architecture and Design, which designed the Liangzhu Experimental School, the Narada Resort and Spa Liangzhu.

Liangzhu New Town is called "the pioneer of urban-supporting service provision" and "Vanke's experimental field". Through this project Vanke planned to become an "urban-supporting service provider". Instead of only providing residential properties, Vanke also tried to deliver related service facilities to fulfil residents' needs for food and entertainment, as well as their spiritual, commercial and public needs. For example, Vanke branded the community cafeteria as "the fifth canteen", beyond the usual canteens in schools and companies, social canteens and the residents' own kitchens. The fifth canteen provides quality, value-for-money food and is popular with older people, children, workers and families who do not have time to cook. It also provides a public place where neighbours can gather together outside of mealtimes.

Box 7.1: Liangzhu New Town "villagers' convention"

1. We are glad to take part in the public activities of the town.

2. Greet neighbours proactively.

3. We protect children's self-esteem and avoid blame in public.

4. Instruct our own kids when a conflict happens between children.

5. Look after neighbours' houses when they are out for a long time. Inform the management centre immediately if any unusual situation happens.

6. We are glad to provide support and help when our neighbours need cooperation in building maintenance.

7. We properly keep and return clothing dropped from balconies upstairs in time.

8. We never litter out of windows, and avoid water dripping from balconies upstairs.

9. We speak in a lower voice in public areas of the town.

10. We turn down indoor stereo systems in the early morning and at night.

11. We dress and behave properly in public.

12. We queue up to get on buses and when shopping, respecting the old and caring for the young.

13. We set off fireworks in designated places at festivals, and ask the management centre for permission during normal times.

14. We avoid disturbing public order and the environment for weddings, funerals or other traditions.

15. We do not sound the horn when driving in the town. We turn down the stereo before rolling down car windows and mute the antitheft device after parking.

16. We drive slowly in the village, avoid using headlights on full beam and give way to pedestrians.

17. We park in specific locations: no crossing the lines or on the lines. Park in the right direction and turn off the ignition after parking.

18. We call for the use of bicycles, electric vehicles or buses when out in the village.

19. Keep the park, the paths and other public areas clean, and take away your litter.

20. We sort household garbage.

21. We call for you to bring your own food packing box when eating out in the town.

22. We prepare reusable bags or bamboo baskets for shopping.

23. Sell unneeded things in the flea market of the village or donate them.

24. We do not set free or raise animals nor grow plants in public areas without agreement.

25. We get legal certificates for our pets and provide them with regular vaccinations.

26. Walk dogs with leads and clear their excrement; never take pets to indoor public places; and put muzzles on aggressive pets.

In Liangzhu, Vanke also helped promote and facilitate the "Liangzhu villagers' convention" (see Box 7.1). The announcement of the villagers' convention was one of the most important events for Liangzhu New Town. It stemmed not from a regulation enforced by Vanke property management, but from a request proposed by residents. Discussions were held to establish a set of rules for better living. 93.7% of residents provided feedback, and 26 out of 50 drafted articles were selected to form the convention. The articles are there to act as guidance for residents' appropriate behaviours. Vanke helped engrave the articles on a notice board in the village plaza.

In 2013, following the success of Liangzhu, Vanke promoted "villagers' conventions" in five other locations in order to enhance neighbourhood harmony and create community trust for "good neighbourhoods, good service and good communities".

7.6.3 Crisis management

Vanke also gets involved in solving customer problems, as shown in the following two examples.

7.6.3.1 Wuhan garbage dump

In April 2001, Vanke signed a contract with the Wuhan Donghu district government to purchase a tract of residential land. The local government promised to close down the nearby garbage dump, about 1 km away from the site, within three years of the deal. The first houses went on sale in 2002. Early buyers complained about the garbage issue in the "Vanke Forum" (an online public space for Vanke customers), asking that Vanke solve the problem as soon as possible. By summer 2003 the whole project was complete, but the garbage dump still existed and had even expanded. The hot summer winds and smoke from fires created by waste pickers in their search for copper seriously affected residents' lives. Vanke Wuhan explained to owners that the government had agreed to close the site down in the near future, and residents accepted this.

In April 2004 rumours spread that the local government could not find a new landfill and the site would remain open. Even worse, it was rumoured that the government planned to turn the site into a garbage transfer station which would remain in use for 30 years – the whole city's garbage would pass through the garbage dump and then be transported to a further landfill site. Large numbers of property owners went on strike.

Wang Shi paid a visit to the owners. After listening to their protests he decided that, no matter how hard it was, Vanke should help the owners solve the problem. In May a customer relationship representative arrived in Wuhan, who provided free screens for windows to help keep the air clean. He also worked proactively with the local government to search for a new landfill site, and communicated with the local press to make sure the process was transparent.

After several months, a Vanke employee found out that the garbage dump was sponsored by the WHO (World Health Organization), which usually has good design standards. Once a truckload of garbage arrived, it should be covered at once by a layer of clay. However, to save costs, this standard was not being strictly followed and the clay cover was being omitted. On a temporary basis, Vanke took charge of the site, purchased clay and made itself responsible for coverage, and also provided compensation for the waste pickers. During the following year the local government found a new landfill site, and the issue was finally closed. Vanke Wuhan staff and the owners planted five acres of trees on the old garbage dump.

The issue brought forth a new culture and rule for Vanke: to be aware of all possible adverse factors beyond the red line (the boundary line of the building). When selling products, Vanke must remind the buyers of all problems within the planning area and 1 km beyond the project red line, both in written and oral form. Wang Shi wrote in his book (*Da dao dang ran*, 大道当然), "One per cent of our mistakes will cause the customer a 100% loss. The most important indicator to measure our success is the level of our customer satisfaction."

7.6.3.2 The flooring incident

In mid-February 2012, an online article claimed that one of Vanke's wood flooring suppliers provided flooring with excessive levels of formaldehyde, and that there was misconduct among Vanke purchasing employees and the supplier, which led to "poison flooring" being installed in several Vanke properties. The article, "Vanke Poison Flooring", quickly spread, and was widely cited in the press and known by the public. Formaldehyde is a sensitive word for many Chinese, who believe that excessive exposure can lead to cancer.

The supplier in question was ranked third by quantity supplied in Vanke's flooring purchasing system, but the same flooring was also widely used by other big developers. If the allegations were founded, then other developers should also have been affected, although none of them was mentioned by the press. Nonetheless, Vanke chose to face the problem by itself. Six hours after the article was posted, Vanke made an announcement: the company would immediately investigate the flooring and internal purchasing processes, and customers and the public would receive timely updates. It would also suspend procurement from the supplier. Flooring purchased but not yet installed would be embargoed in stock; for the flooring already installed, Vanke would invite third-party inspectors to examine the situation.

In total, 72 samples from 16 cities were tested by 17 different authorities: 41 samples from installed properties, 22 from storage, three from delivered but not installed products and six from prototype rooms. Of the 72 samples, one was found in Foshan New City Bay with formaldehyde emissions 1.9 mg/litre, which exceeded the government standard of 1.5 mg/litre. The flooring had been used in 104 units with 25 households already moved in. Vanke Foshan immediately announced plans to help customers replace the flooring and compensate them for any related damage.

Typically a quality check tested three samples; if the first tested was within the limits, then a pass was awarded; if the first test failed, then the remaining two would be tested with the majority results determined as the final result. Vanke, however, declared a fail result if the first test showed excessive levels. Even if later the remaining two samples passed, Wang Shi believed that his management team needed to admit faults and learn, so as to avoid further mistakes in future. "The incident acted as a cold to test Vanke's overall immune system," Wang Shi wrote in his book. Later, Vanke set up its own quality control facilities in its research lab.

7.7 The final word

On 13 November 2014, Vanke officially announced that it was joining the WWF Climate Savers programme, and was the world's first real estate company to take part. Vanke publicly set specific and comprehensive targets for reducing emissions. Vanke expected that by the end of 2018 it would:

- Reduce cumulative emissions by 1.46 million tons CO_2e (carbon dioxide equivalent) by increasing industrialized housing technologies and developing industrialized houses of 49 million m^2 floor space

- Reduce cumulative emissions by 2.56 million CO_2e by developing three-star Green housing with an annual growth rate no less than 15% and with building space at least 13.5 million m^2

- Reduce cumulative emissions by 1.28 million CO_2e by installing more than 0.56 million m^2 solar water heating systems on new residential buildings

In addition, Vanke committed to providing free access for other developers to its existing industrialized housing patents. Mr Mao Daqing, former Senior Vice President of Vanke said:

> We believe only the industry-leading companies that take more responsibilities can lead the whole industry to reduce its carbon footprint … we set ambitious targets for our supply chain and business operation … we also hope to promote change in our partners.

Along with this strategy, Vanke is also feeling the pressure from its less proactive competitors (green strategies usually mean higher costs). In 2014, Vanke's sales were only RMB 4 billion more than the second-largest developer, Green Land Group. The gap was RMB 8.4 billion in 2013, RMB 36.2 billion in 2012 and 43.9 billion in 2011. Moving from focusing solely on residential real estate, Vanke is trying to reposition itself as an "urban-supporting service provider", fulfilling urban business and public needs. In January 2013 Vanke set up its commercial real estate business unit focusing on three product lines:

1. Community business – fulfilling the most basic living needs

2. Living plaza – a store cluster which covers several communities

3. City malls, with a large amount of integrated commercial projects

In 2014, Vanke started to deliver various new products such as rental apartments, office properties, ageing services and tourism services. All these developments may be the way forward for Vanke.

7.8 Case summary

Vanke, the world's largest residential property developer, also believes it should be a leader in sustainability practices. In promoting its green vision, however, Vanke faces a number of challenges. In particular, it must balance the need to provide high-quality, affordable housing for people utilizing environmentally and socially sustainable practices, all without impacting too heavily on costs.

Vanke has responded to this challenge by positioning itself as an "urban-supporting service provider".

At Liangzhu New Town near the city of Hangzhou, Vanke has introduced innovative facilities to cater for people's physical, spiritual, commercial and public needs. An example is the Fifth Canteen, which:

- Provides quality, value-for-money food

- Is popular with old people, children, workers and families who do not have time to cook

- Provides a public space where people can gather outside of mealtimes

- Acts not only as a provider of food, but as a community hub which caters to people's social and spiritual needs

- Draws the community together in a way that ordinary real estate developments do not

8
Towards sustainable mobility: Volvo Group

8.1 Introduction

Volvo is a Swedish automobile manufacturer founded in 1927, in Gothenburg, Sweden. "Cars are driven by people. The guiding principle behind everything we make at Volvo, therefore, is and must remain, safety," declared the founders Assar Gabrielsson and Gustav Larson.[1]

Today the Volvo Group has more than 100,000 employees in 58 countries. After the sale of Volvo Cars in 1999, the group has focused on its commercial vehicles business. Trucks are a large part of that vehicle business. Volvo Group acquired Renault Trucks, Mack Trucks and the Japanese company UD Trucks, and established

---

1   Volvo is famous for its high safety standards. Owners are proud of achieving high mileage; one well-documented 1966 Volvo P1800 has been driven over 2.8 million miles, a Guinness World Record for most miles driven by a single owner in a non-commercial vehicle. According to some figures, the average age of a Volvo at time of being scrapped is 19.8 years (second only to Mercedes).

a joint venture with India Eicher to manufacture trucks in India. Other products include construction equipment, vehicles on-site, coaches, buses and special marine and industrial engines.

Volvo Group is continually evolving new engine technologies that reduce emissions, especially nitrogen oxide and particulate matter. Their policy is that each new product developed should be more sustainable than the one it replaces. Volvo is also aiming to reduce the impact of its production operations by reducing energy consumption and CO_2 emissions. In 2007, Volvo opened the world's first carbon neutral automotive plant in Ghent, Belgium. The long-term ambition is to make all plants CO_2 neutral. "This is not an easy undertaking," said former Volvo Group CEO Leif Johansson,[2] "but we are prepared to try different alternatives to achieve our goal for CO_2-free production in our plants."

At the Ghent plant Volvo decided to construct three wind power plants on the site. These supply half of the plant's electricity requirements. The remainder is certified green energy supplied by the Belgium energy company Electrabel. A new pellet-fired biomass plant supplies 70% of the heating requirements for the Ghent plant, and energy for the combustion process is provided by solar cells on the roof of the building. The remaining 30% is provided by an oil-fired boiler converted to burn bio-oil. The Ghent plant has an annual production of 35,000 trucks and employs 2,500 people. Other plants, including truck plants in Gothenburg, Tuve and Umeå, all in Sweden, have followed or are preparing to follow the Ghent example.

Even during the world financial crisis of 2008, Volvo Group did not reduce investment in R&D on environmental protection. The company reduced spending on advertising, travel and promotion, focusing instead on its three core values: quality, safety and

2   Leif Johansson left Volvo in September 2011.

environmental protection. Annually, 3–4% of the group's sales are invested in R&D, and most of this investment has been focused on improvements in engines, engine-related technologies and alternative fuel sources.

This case study discusses how Volvo Group is finding new innovative solutions to create sustainable transport systems. It focuses particularly on the corporate challenges and achievements of Volvo in China, where the 12th Five-Year Plan has a strong focus on energy saving, climate change and environmental issues.

8.2 Volvo Group in China

Volvo Group entered the Chinese market by establishing a representative office in Beijing in 1992. At the end of the 1990s Volvo Group had strengthened its corporate investment in China and had established joint ventures. Today Volvo Group China is a very diverse business with nearly 5,000 employees.

Although the truck business accounts for a large part of the Volvo Group's global business, in China the strong local demand for basic infrastructure construction means that construction equipment accounts for more than 80% of Volvo's business there. In Shandong Province, Volvo invested in the local company Shandong Lingong Construction Machinery. The plant in Shanghai employs 430 people and manufactures excavators. Since establishment in 2003, capacity has increased fourfold from the original design. Volvo Group also has a wholly-owned production factory in Shanghai Pudong, a joint venture enterprise in Linyi and a production base in Shandong Lingong. The plant in Linyi employs 220–230 people and produces road-building equipment.

Robert Li, General Manager and Vice President of Operations for Volvo Group China, explains that Volvo chose to set up plants in and near Shanghai because the infrastructure and logistics systems were better developed there than elsewhere in China, and there was also a "talent pool" of potential employees. "In terms of cost, Shanghai was not expensive at all," he says.

In addition to the three construction machinery plants, Volvo Group has two joint venture companies engaged in bus production in China: Silverbus, based in Xi'an and producing long-distance coaches, and Sunwin bus, based in Shanghai. Volvo Penta, which also has its factory in Shanghai, makes and sells industrial and marine engines. The truck business consists mostly of a sales office located in Beijing, though there is a joint venture company part-owned by Volvo subsidiary UD Truck in Hangzhou. There is also an R&D centre in Jinan, Shandong and a purchasing centre in Shanghai. This case study focuses on the construction machinery, as it is the largest and most important part of Volvo Group China's portfolio.

8.3 Volvo Group China's environmental solutions

> For the first time there is now a commercially viable hybrid bus on the market, the Volvo 7700 Hybrid. With up to 30% lower fuel consumption and hybrid components from Volvo, bus operators can earn a payback on the extra cost in only five to seven years. The lower fuel consumption reduces the emission of the greenhouse gas CO_2 by up to 30%. The discharge of particles and nitrous oxides declines by up to 40–50% compared with the diesel version.
>
> Volvo news release

Efficient transport plays a crucial role in the development of most societies and economies. At the same time, however, transport has a negative impact on the environment, not least in the form of emissions. The Volvo Group has made the reduction of negative environmental impact a priority. Volvo does this by taking the environmental impact into account at all stages of the product life-cycle, from the first sketches on the drawing board throughout the product's service life and on until the product has fulfilled its purpose and is recycled.

The Volvo hybrid bus mentioned above is an example of this. A significant reason why fuel savings of up to 30% can be achieved is that all hybrid components are developed by Volvo itself. "The common approach has been that bus manufacturers purchased hybrid components externally and attempted to adapt them to their own bus, but this is difficult," says Håkan Karlsson, President of Volvo Bus Corporation. "We developed the components internally, and therefore we have been able to optimize the bus's fuel consumption fully. This also ensures very high reliability."

Another feature of Volvo's hybrid technology is that the diesel engine is switched off at bus stops and traffic lights. "When the bus then starts moving it is driven by the electric motor," says Karlsson, "and when the bus reaches 15–20 kph, the diesel engine starts up automatically." This means that in cities, passengers, pedestrians and fellow road-users are spared from noise and exhaust fumes.

For all of its plants in China, Volvo has set very high sustainability standards. It is a general rule that even in joint ventures all members of the Volvo Group must meet its corporate environmental protection standards, which are set higher than those set by either international standard organizations or the Chinese government.

Volvo Group has a special organizational system consisting of Business Areas and Business Units. Business Areas work face to face with customers. "These include truck brands such as Volvo Truck, Renault and UD Truck," explains Stella Ye, Chassis Group Purchasing Manager. "Apart from the truck brands, we also have

Volvo Construction, Volvo Bus, Volvo Financial Services and Volvo Penta, all of which also face end-users. Each of these is a Business Area." Volvo Business Units are responsible for supporting the Business Areas through the "3Ps": product development, product planning and purchasing. Stella Ye, for example, is in charge of supporting all product development and product R&D related to truck brands, including costs and the choice of suppliers. Volvo also has a Quality, Environment and Safety (QES) department which includes specialized engineers responsible for solving problems. If a problem cannot be solved in-house, Volvo will seek help and cooperation from academic institutions such as Tsinghua University, with whom Volvo has set up a "Green Economy and Sustainable Development Research Centre".[3]

As part of its vendor evaluation process, Volvo focuses strongly on environmental protection. Volvo is one of the first truck companies to require suppliers to provide environment-related certification for areas such as energy saving. If suppliers cannot provide certificates, Volvo asks them to provide action plans and confirm when they will reach certification. Volvo also asked suppliers to do environmental self-assessment. "Environmental care is an important part of our mission. If a potential supplier cannot meet our requirements, then we will not choose him as a supplier," says Stella Ye.

8.4 Innovations in logistics to reduce CO_2 emissions

Volvo Group China is noteworthy for two particular types of innovation in recent years. These are:

---

3   See http://auto.people.com.cn/n/2015/0323/c1005-26736686.html (in Chinese).

1. Innovations in logistics to reduce CO_2 emissions

2. Innovations in packaging to reduce waste

8.4.1 Volvo global practice in packaging: Volvo Emballage

The fundamental solution to the above challenges lies in the implementation of a standardized system in logistics (e.g. packaging, certification, ICT and best practice). Among them, standardized packaging poses the greatest challenge but could have a great positive impact on the environment. The Volvo Group has been attempting to implement standardized packaging in China since its first entry into the market.

In fact, Volvo has been an innovator in packaging since the 1950s. At that time, Volvo truck and car plants were individually responsible for packaging, with a special department to manage the recycling of packaging. Volvo Logistics has since taken on responsibility for all packaging and now uses a waste-reduction system called "Volvo Emballage", which uses recyclable wooden pallets.[4] The pallets can be stored in Volvo's major plants and by suppliers in different countries. After the packaging is transported to the plants, it can be either returned or reused. If the plants want to continue using the packaging, they can hire it from Volvo Logistics China. This way, suppliers will not have to use additional carton packaging. "This is an obvious example of Volvo's environmental protection and emissions reduction procedures," says Stella Ye. "Originally, the production, scrappage and disposal of wooden boxes all had costs, and had an impact on environment. The Emballage system is cheaper. But the positive impact on the environment is more important than cost."

---

4   In Swedish, *emballage* literally means "pallet".

The Emballage system is described as follows: planar dimensions of packages are designed according to the product. For each component, there is a corresponding detailed standard packaging specification. If it is a big product, the planar dimension of the package would be twice that of the pallet. If it is a small part, the planar dimension could be one-half, one-quarter or even one-eighth that of the pallet. This design is convenient for stacking. The height of the packaging is also very flexible. Normal plastic boxes are all rectangular, but Volvo plastic boxes are trapezoidal, which makes them easier to warehouse and transport. This reduces delivery costs and maximizes use of the storage space. Volvo packaging can be circulated and used globally either by Volvo or its suppliers/customers, which saves on packaging materials.

8.4.2 The situation in China: logistics challenges

Logistics within Volvo Group China comprises three major activities: warehousing, delivery and land transportation. The company uses agents for the importation of raw materials, and logistics is only responsible for delivering parts to the factory. Volvo Group China has its own fleet of vehicles to deliver to the various sites. After being repackaged, finished products are shipped. "We've got the logistics planning capacity in-house but outsourced operational activities," says Lansi Jiang, Vice President for Corporate Communications and Brand for Volvo Group China. According to her, this is because logistics planning is one of Volvo's core competences, and Volvo makes profits from the operation.

Volvo Logistics is a subsidiary of the Volvo Group, and provides automotive logistics services to internal and external departments. Volvo China Logistic Services is divided into three areas of activity. One is "inbound logistics", the delivery of parts from suppliers to Volvo. The second is "outbound logistics", the warehousing and

logistics of the whole vehicle and related items. The third one is
"recyclable packages". This packaging system uses wood, metal or
plastic packaging which can be recycled many times and circulated
globally. Volvo China Logistics Services has its headquarters in
Shanghai with offices in Beijing, Linyi and Chongqing. It employs
around 50 people, mostly based in Shanghai.

Ying Wang, Purchasing Manager of Volvo Logistics China, who
worked in the Volvo Group China packaging department from 2004
to 2009, explained that:

> Although we are the logistics company within the Volvo
> Group, we do not handle real logistics operations such as ship-
> ping and air transport. We have such departments as customs,
> risk management, accounting and finance, but otherwise we
> outsource to professional transportation companies. My job is
> to purchase these transportation services.

At Volvo, packaging is distributed to suppliers according to their
requirements. If the suppliers want to continue to use the packaging, they in turn can package parts to delivery to the assembly
plants. If the packaging is no longer needed, it is sent back to
Volvo's warehouse.

In China, Volvo found that some of its suppliers were not totally
comfortable with using Volvo's packaging system. Volvo Group
China does not charge for its packaging but suppliers have to guarantee that the company's packaging will be stored and operated
in the right way to avoid excessive loss and damage. To find effective solutions to logistics problems arising from the suppliers, Volvo
Group China assigns a quality inspector. If a supplier makes many
mistakes, the inspector will visit more frequently in order to assess
the situation and provide training. The Volvo Group tries to improve
suppliers' operational procedures step-by-step and explains what
benefits they might gain by using Volvo's packaging.

We can take an example from one of the suppliers to the Volvo Construction Machinery Plant in Linyi. This supplier is relatively small; it manufactures cast iron parts and welding components. The component it supplies is not particularly large but is quite heavy. Volvo Group China invited this supplier to its premises to explain the procedures. Ying Wang explained:

> During the early stages of the process, it seemed there were no problems. They came to learn how we operate, and then we sent the packaging according to the agreement signed. During the trial period, everything was fine. However, after a few months, we found that the packaging coming back from this supplier had very high damage rates, more than maximum limit we had expected.

To solve the problem, Volvo Group China sent inspectors to the supplier's factory. The inspector discovered that some of the operations – including parts loading – had not met Volvo's requirements. As the weight of a single part was relatively high, the packaging was more likely to be damaged during loading. The inspectors listed all the improper operations and gave suggestions. As a result, performance improved and damage rates declined.

The underlying reason for the difficulty detailed in the above story lay in the fact that the logistics standardization level in China was very low – including the standardization of wooden and plastic packaging (some suppliers used their own packaging) and the standardization of loading them into trucks. Volvo had to train workers and suppliers on how to use the packaging more effectively. Assembly workers felt uncomfortable with the changes. "In the EU and the USA the level of standardization is high, but this is not the case in China. We have to educate one supplier after another. This is time-consuming and difficult to do. This is the biggest challenge we face in packaging," says Ying Wang.

More generally, packaging is a societal issue for Volvo Group China. When the Volvo Group starts working with a new supplier in Europe, the company might find out that the supplier also collaborates with Mercedes and Evco. Those companies have their own requirements for standardization, which may be different from those of Volvo. Volvo would then invite a number of suppliers to sit down together and talk through corporate requirements and procedures. In Europe, Volvo has fewer than 60 people managing 2,700 suppliers. However, in China the same principle does not apply. Volvo needs not only to invite suppliers to its own plants but also to visit them at theirs. Ying Wang says:

> We can't ensure standardization among so many suppliers. We simply don't have enough people to do this. That's why it [the Emballage system] is difficult to implement in China. There is a huge gap between Europe and China. In China, we only have 70 suppliers that use this packaging. We only increase this number by 10–20 suppliers per year. When one of our plants in Linyi was relocated, we had to implement our procedures among 18 suppliers. It took us a year and a half to reach the damage level we expected.[5]

Related to the standardization of packaging, there is a low level of standardization across the logistics industry in general. Volvo Group China ran into problems with setting routes and times for milk runs (regular collection and delivery from suppliers). Road conditions in China are difficult and traffic jams affect punctuality. Also, suppliers' on-time stocking rates tend to be low. If vehicles go to pick up the parts but the supplier is not ready yet to hand them over, this affects the pickup from the next supplier. To encourage punctual delivery, Volvo Group China applies local penalty rates,

5   Volvo has set an upper limit for packaging damage. Once the damage rate reaches this level, supplier development activities by quality inspectors are triggered.

telling suppliers that if delays affect production processes they may charge 8,000 yuan per minute or 1.5 million per hour to compensate. Yet there are still large numbers of delays.

A second challenges lies in the Internet interface system. Suppliers need a user password to log into the system. They can then search for the information they want, make orders and exchange inventory information. When they are ready to deliver, they can input data through this Internet interface. However, since the Volvo interface is designed in English, Chinese suppliers encounter communication problems. Volvo has found that for those suppliers who have a low level of English comprehension, it takes around half a year to understand all the functions.

Last but not least is the issue of compliance with international quality, safety and environmental certification, in addition to the Volvo Group's quality standards. Very few Chinese suppliers can reach the standards set by Volvo. For example, the Volvo Group requires its European suppliers to have ISO 9000 and ISO 14000 certificates, and has special requirements for suppliers' trucks and emissions. Volvo's suppliers all have monitoring systems and provide the Volvo Group with their emission reports regularly. This way, Volvo can ensure that they can work together with its suppliers to reduce CO_2 emissions. Some Chinese companies can achieve ISO 9000, but it is generally recognized by the Chinese companies that achieving ISO 14000 is more difficult than achieving ISO 9000 because costs may rise if more environmentally friendly materials and processes lead to higher production costs; also, investment in fixed capital may rise if a company must implement pollution reduction equipment.[6]

6   ISO 9000 is a quality management standard, and ISO 14000 sets out the criteria for an environmental management system (EMS). ISO 9000 certification is performed by third-party organizations rather than being awarded by ISO directly. Hence, it is more difficult and time-consuming to obtain ISO 14000 than ISO 9000.

"If you talk to Chinese suppliers about emission reductions, they treat it as a joke. At the moment, they have no idea how many emissions they even produce," says Ying Wang.

The Volvo Group gives its suppliers time to achieve certification in China. As long as a supplier can achieve the certification at some point Volvo will sign a contract with them, because the company is aware that many suppliers actively apply for ISO certificates only after they have signed contracts. But this has still been a major challenge for Volvo. As part of finding a solution, Volvo is doing a pilot programme with a Chinese supplier, requiring daily reporting on the supplier's mileage, fuel consumption and load capacity to calculate its CO_2 emission. If this project proves successful then Volvo will gradually apply this policy to other suppliers.

8.4.3 A Chinese solution for packaging

Recycling of cartons and non-metal waste was another important environmental issue in the early days of the Volvo Group's entry into the Chinese market. Before 2009 many parts came from overseas and needed to be unpacked. The discarded packaging included cartons, iron sheet, timbers and plastics, which were treated as solid waste. This contradicts one of the Volvo Group's three core values: protection for the environment. "Environmental protection is our responsibility," said Robert Li:

> But now we have used returnable racks for domestically manufactured parts since 2009. The racks are made of metal and have wheels, enabling movement on-site. For example, pipes can be put either in wooden crates or in cartons. These items of packaging were formerly removed and treated as waste. We realized that if we used returnable racks, we could put the pipes on the racks and send them to the plants. The racks could then be returned to suppliers after use. We didn't need packaging at all.

This approach to packaging had a number of effects on the company. For example:

- The trucks used to transport the waste for recycling produced CO_2 emissions. The packaging waste also occupied space when being stored while awaiting recycling, thus reducing warehouse and site efficiency.

- The disposal of waste incurred human resource costs.

- Packaging increased the space occupied by parts at the warehouse, and there were also labour costs involved in removing the packaging.

In order to reduce unnecessary packaging or get rid of packaging completely, after careful assessment and research Volvo Group China came up with an effective solution. Solid waste packaging was replaced with returnable (tote) racks, which comply with the parts' protection, movement and production rules and remove waste completely.

Guided by this principle, Volvo Group China set up a returnable shelf improvement team with members from engineering, logistics, purchasing, quality and production. They used parts manufactured by local suppliers to test this idea. The purchasing department communicated the packaging requirements with parts suppliers. The suppliers and Volvo Group China engineering staff then worked together to design the tote shelf and slip groove for different parts, to make sure the racks could protect the parts during transportation. The newly designed racks were then tested for their feasibility and effectiveness.

The Volvo Group became a WWF Climate Saver in October 2010. Currently, there are four brands of trucks (i.e. UD, Renault, Mack and Terex) within the Volvo Group that have joined the Climate Savers programme. The next step is to add Volvo's construction machinery business to the project. "This is going to be a huge investment. To create a zero emission plant needs vast investment," says Lansi Jiang.

The Volvo Group has also worked hard to increase employee and public awareness. For example, Volvo IT developed special software which can be connected with staff mobile phones to calculate their daily carbon footprint. At the 2011 Auto Show in Shanghai, Volvo Group China distributed small gifts to raise awareness of carbon emissions.

8.4.4 Impact on societies: educating customers

The 2011 Volvo Trucks Fuelwatch Competition Final Award Ceremony was held at The Palace in Beijing, along with the Volvo Trucks Family Day carnival-themed "Environmental Protection" drive. During the event, Volvo Trucks officially announced that Chinese customers could now order trucks equipped with Volvo's state-of-the-art Euro IV engines.[7] This industry-first announcement emphasized Volvo Trucks' commitment to China, promoting a healthy and sustainable development of the Chinese transport and logistics industry.

Volvo Trucks was the first commercial vehicle company to conduct such an event to popularize advanced technology and products, including energy-saving and hybrid technology. In addition, fuel-efficient driving and the concept of environmental care were also promoted among drivers and logistics companies. The Volvo Trucks Fuelwatch Competition advances drivers' skills and supports them to achieve optimum fuel consumption, thereby allowing customers to improve efficiency and strengthen their economic returns. The

---

7   European emission standards (EMS) define the acceptable limits for exhaust emissions of new vehicles sold in EU member states. Here it signifies EMS 4 for trucks and buses.

truck drivers were provided with training before and during the competition, and were asked to drive the truck following a number of predesigned movements to test their driving skills. Since its debut in 2009, the Volvo Trucks Fuelwatch Competition has been widely recognized across the Chinese truck industry for its energy-saving efforts and humanitarian care for drivers.

As an expert on road transport, Volvo Trucks has used a "Total Transportation Solutions" strategy in China since 1999. This is a sophisticated programme to improve the efficiency of logistics, including consulting, maintenance and training. The promotion and application of eco-friendly technology and concepts are among the solutions. Volvo Trucks is the field leader in the research and development of hybrid and fuel efficiency products, and has achieved good results. In some developed countries, Volvo Trucks has already started to market Euro IV and V products. With the entry of its Euro IV products in China, Volvo Trucks' total solutions strategy will gather pace in the market.

Joachim Rosenberg, President of Volvo (China) Investment Co., Ltd, said at the event:

> Environmental care is one of our three core values at Volvo Trucks and it has been this way for almost 40 years. We do not shy away from the fact that our industry is a part of the global greenhouse gas issue and therefore it is even more important for us as a company to be part of the solution. When it comes to fuel consumption, for us at Volvo Trucks, every drop counts. During events like this, it is usually the trucks, engines and transmissions that get all the attention and we are of course proud of the fact that we have the most efficient vehicles on the market. More importantly, however, we have also created a holistic approach based on the customer's operations, covering big and small ways of achieving fuel savings. This is good for the customer, for the environment and for society. Our Fuelwatch competition, run for several years now across all major Asian countries, is just one example.

The event was a journey into Volvo Trucks culture, showing the public Volvo's core values of "quality, safety, environmental care", and their connotations. Interactive activities were designed for the public to learn more about the close relationship between trucks and humans regarding safety, the environment and daily life. Volvo Trucks Drivers' Club invites its members and their families to experience the programme and to help them better understand drivers' work and values. Volvo Trucks wants to spread its green ideas all through society, to form a greater force in environmental protection which will require everybody's contribution.

Eric Labat, President of Volvo Trucks in China, said:

> In the last few years, we have developed this approach in China and we can proudly say that we are one of the industry leaders. Volvo has a very clear strategy, a long-term commitment and high ambitions concerning the booming Chinese market. Our idea is to work with government and transport companies to undertake sustainable development in R&D, manufacturing, application and recycling. We hope that more and more people will join us as we try to build a brighter future for us all.

8.5 Volvo Group China sustainable innovation: barriers, enablers and lessons learned

While introducing sustainable innovations in China, the Volvo Group encountered a number of different barriers and enablers. Some of them have already been described. As Lansi Jiang sums up:

> Supply chain members, scholars and experts need to work together to get things done. Industry associations in China are also considered part of the government. The media is also important, because it provides the channels to promote good practice. Industry associations are more willing to elect the greenest company and greenest products and assume positive

roles to promote environmental protection activities. Furthermore, China's Development and Reform Commission (CDRC)
and Ministry of Commerce will make plans tailored to the
domestic situation.

Volvo's core value (protecting the environment) is already "deeply
embedded in employees' mind-sets", according to Lansi Jiang. In
each process, from raw material to manufacturing, this value is
always present in the minds of Volvo employees. Thus from this
point of view, there is very little resistance. Also important is the
fact that in recent years the Volvo Group has developed steadily,
both in China and globally. This means that Volvo has the financial resources and capabilities to invest in environmental protection
activities.

One of the lessons learned so far by Volvo is that everybody
needs to be committed. Volvo has put in a lot of resources to implement its core value of environmental protection. In doing so, Volvo
has provided more promotion and education at employee level
and supplier level to increase environmental awareness. This is not
just a verbal commitment; Volvo takes action and supplies a lot of
investment. There is also a realization that, in order to address its
environmental targets, the Volvo Group has to operate efficiently
and effectively; otherwise there would not be enough capacity and
financial resources to meet the targets.

Perhaps surprisingly, one factor that favours Volvo in China is, as
Yun Jiang, WWF Climate Savers Senior Programme Officer puts it:

> Some of the elements [such as protecting the environment]
> are in the blood of Nordic companies. You feel that they are
> not only financially successful, but are also investing a lot in
> environmental protection. This is sometimes what you don't
> understand from an Asian perspective as it is not the priority.

Lansi Jiang echoes this view:

Sometimes you will feel they have done too much. But if you stay in a Nordic country for some time, you will understand. When [former] President Hu Jintao of China visited Sweden, he insisted on visiting Volvo with two questions: firstly, why does a small country like this have so many companies listed in the Fortune 500? Secondly, in a small country like Sweden, how has it been possible to invest so hugely in environmental protection and achieve so much?

When you visit these countries, you'll find the people there are so natural. They lack natural resources and many would find their living environment to be harsh. Therefore they cherish the resources they have. Second, they have such a small population. Once a company is set up, the first thing on their list is exporting as they don't have a large home market to appeal to. So the spirit of Vikings is in their blood. They don't think doing environmental protection is something extra. They want to do this from the bottom of their hearts. They think this is how this should be done.

However, Vicki Ni, Volvo China's Director of Corporate Communications and Brand, warns of another barrier:

Being environmentally friendly is one of the big advantages of our products and a unique selling point. However, in China there is also a lot of price competition. If we want to reach a strict environmental protection standard, the price of our products will surely have no advantage in comparison with domestic products.

8.6 The final word

Lansi Jiang recollects a well-known speech by a former Volvo Group CEO:

We do manufacture automotives and may have an impact on the environment and carbon emissions. We are part of the problem, but we also want to be an active player in solving the problem. Of course, we hope that we can influence government through our work. Governments should provide some incentive policies such tax benefits to the customers who are willing to purchase environmentally friendly products. After all, the costs of environmentally friendly products are very high. Although our truck may save 30% in fuel, the price also increases by 20% – even 30%. So, to encourage investment in environmentally friendly products, I think some positive policies should be introduced in China.

8.7 Case summary

Volvo Group has made reduction of its environmental impact a priority across all its operations. The policy is that each new product developed should be more sustainable than the one it replaces. In China, Volvo has faced three specific challenges: low levels of standardization of packaging and logistics industry practice; lack of ICT systems; and poor compliance with international quality, safety and environmental certification. Volvo has responded by:

- Providing training on standardization and industry practice to suppliers and helping them develop dedicated personnel

- Persuading suppliers to invest in ICT and providing training for supplier staff

- Giving suppliers time to develop and move towards compliance, encouraging them to learn by doing

- Educating customers about fuel efficiency and establishing programmes to help encourage better fuel efficiency and spread sustainable values

9
Sustainable value chain strategy: Yingli

9.1 Introduction

Yingli Solar is a product brand marketed by the Yingli Green Energy Holding Company Limited (Yingli for short), a leading solar energy company and one of the world's largest vertically integrated photovoltaic (PV) manufacturers. Yingli covers the entire PV value chain, from the production of polysilicon through ingot casting and wafering, to solar cell production and module assembly. Yingli currently maintains a balanced vertically integrated production capacity of 2,450 MW per year at its production facilities located in Baoding, Haikou, Tianjin and Hengshui. Yingli distributes its PV modules to a wide range of markets in over 50 countries and regions worldwide, including Germany, Spain, Italy, Greece, France, South Korea, China and the USA. Headquartered in Baoding, Hebei province in China (one hour by train from Beijing), Yingli has more than 30 subsidiaries and branch offices worldwide. The company was listed on the New York Stock Exchange (NYSE: YGE) in 2007.

Yingli believes its responsibility is to "turn the Sun's boundless power into affordable green energy for all". In 2010, Yingli became the first Chinese company and the first renewable energy company to sponsor the FIFA World Cup in South Africa. In 2014 it again sponsored the FIFA World Cup in Brazil. It supplied PV modules to 2014 FIFA World Cup stadiums including the Maracana Stadium in Rio de Janeiro, making it the cleanest World Cup in history.

Yingli's products are deployed in three market segments: commercial, utility and residential. The majority of net revenues come from the sales of PV modules (98.1% of sales in 2011 and 96.5% in 2012). The remainder come mainly from PV systems which combine modules with batteries, inverters and other third-party equipment.

9.2 PV technology

PV technology has long been acknowledged as a clean energy technology which draws on the planet's most plentiful and widely distributed renewable energy source – the sun. Solar PV is the third most important renewable energy source in terms of globally installed capacity, after hydro and wind power.

PV is a method of converting solar energy into direct current (DC) electricity using semiconducting materials that exhibit the photovoltaic effect. Layers of semiconducting materials are embraced in PV cells, and a PV system employs PV modules composed of a number of PV cells. When light touches the PV cells it creates an electric field across the layers, causing electricity to flow. The greater the intensity of the light is, the greater the flow of electricity. No pollution is emitted during the operation of the PV cells, although environmental impacts may occur during its production stage.

The performance of a solar cell is measured in terms of efficiency at turning sunlight into electricity. A typical commercial solar module has an efficiency of 16.5%, which means around one-sixth of the sunlight striking the module is converted into electricity. Increasing solar module efficiencies is an important goal for the PV industry, which means holding down the cost per cell.

Currently there are two main commercialized PV technologies: crystalline silicon (monocrystalline or polycrystalline) and thin film. Crystalline silicon is made from thin slices cut from a single crystal of silicon (monocrystalline) or from a block of silicon crystals (polycrystalline). Monocrystalline panels normally have a better performance than polycrystalline panels: the former have an average conversion efficiency of 15–20%, and the latter 13–16%. Crystalline silicon PV technology currently represents about 90% of the market because of its extensive manufacturing base and high conversion efficiency. Thin film is made by depositing extremely thin layers of photosensitive materials onto a low-cost backing such as glass, stainless steel or plastic. Thin film is cheaper to produce, which counterbalances the technology's lower conversion efficiency rates: 10–15% on average.

The first practical application of PV was to power orbiting satellites and other spacecraft. Today, the majority of PV modules are used for grid-connected power generation. An inverter is used in the process to convert DC into AC (alternating current). AC is the form in which electric power is delivered to businesses and residences.

As described by the EPIA (European Photovoltaic Industry Association), PV applications can include residential systems, larger industrial/commercial systems and utility-scale power plants, and also consumer goods. A solar PV system can be either connected to the grid or off-grid. PV applications mainly include grid-connected power plants, grid-connected residential systems, off-grid systems

Grid-connected power plants	Can be ground-mounted, or located on large industrial/commercial buildings such as shopping malls, airport terminals or railway stations. These produce a large quantity of PV electricity at a single point, and make use of already available space providing a part of the electricity needed by these energy-intensive consumers (in the case of industrial/commercial buildings).
Grid-connected residential systems	Can be rooftop, integrated in the building's envelope (used as a building component for insulation, roofing tile, shading, etc.) or mounted directly on the ground (in the garden). Connection to the local electricity network allows any excess power produced to feed the electricity grid and to sell it to the utility. Electricity is imported from the network when there is no sun.
Off-grid systems for rural electrification	Can be a small solar PV system covering the basic electricity needs of a household, or a larger solar mini-plant, providing enough power for several homes. These systems bring access to electricity to remote areas (mountain huts, developing countries, small islands).
Off-grid industrial applications	Very frequent in the telecommunications and transport fields: repeater stations for mobile phones, traffic signals, marine navigation aids, security phones, remote lighting, highway signs, etc. These bring cost-effective power in areas far away from the electricity grid, avoiding the high cost of installing cabled networks.
Consumer goods	Many everyday electrical appliances use PV cells: watches, calculators, toys, battery chargers, water sprinklers, lighting, etc.

TABLE 9.1   PV applications

Source: http://www.epia.org/about-us/about-photovoltaics/solar-photovoltaic-technology/.

for rural electrification, off-grid industrial applications and consumer goods (Table 9.1 gives more details for each type).

9.3 PV value chain and distribution

A PV value chain includes three streams and five parts (see Figure 9.1), the upstream: polysilicon materials and ingot/wafer production; midstream: solar cell and PV module production; and downstream: PV deployment.

- **Polysilicon production.** Polysilicon production converts metallurgical-grade silicon to polysilicon that can be used

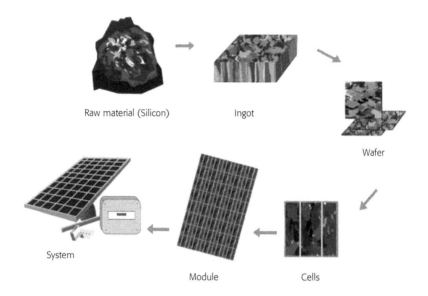

FIGURE 9.1   PV value chain

for solar cells. Polysilicon production is both capital and energy intensive. The first step is to place silicon dioxide into an electric arc furnace and then yield silicon with 1% impurity. The 99% pure silicon, called polysilicon material, is purified even further by dragging the impurities towards one end with each pass. At a specific point, the impure end is removed and the rest becomes pure seed crystal of silicon. Next, a seed crystal of silicon is dipped into melted polycrystalline silicon.

- **Ingot/wafer production.** As the seed crystal is withdrawn and rotated, a cylindrical ingot is formed. An ingot can be a single crystal, called monosilicon, or multiple silicon crystals, called polysilicon. Next, cylindrical ingots are sliced into thin layers called wafers. The wafers can be of circular, rectangular or hexagonal shape and are ready to be fitted together to become the surface of the solar cell.

- **Solar cell.** At this stage, the wafer surface is rough-etched by liquid acid to reduce the reflectivity of incident light and raise efficiency. Phosphorus gas is then injected into the wafer, resulting in P-N junction for the photovoltaic effect. Next, a silicon nitride antireflective coating is created on the wafer surface. Finally, the silver and aluminium slurry are used to screen print on both surfaces of the wafer.

- **PV module production.** Finished solar cells are sealed into silicon rubber and placed into metal frames with multiple layers of glasses and plastic to form a module.

- **PV deployment.** A PV system includes PV modules and BOS (balance of system) components. BOS components mainly include solar panel mounting equipment, a PV charge controller, PV current monitoring devices, inverters, cables and wiring, connectors, overcurrent protection, combiner boxes, grounding hardware and lightning protection equipment. The inverter is the most significant part of the BOS components. PV deployment refers to the integration of the PV systems and the delivery of solar electricity to final users. The deployment process includes system design, system installation construction, operation and maintenance and repair services.

Generally in the PV value chain, the upstream achieves the highest profit while the downstream achieves the second highest profits, with the midstream achieving the lowest profits. Polysilicon production used to be dominated by firms in technologically advanced countries such as Wacker Chemie AG (Wacker) in Germany and OCI in South Korea. Wacker produces hyper-pure polysilicon for use in electronic and solar wafers, while OCI imports raw materials from China and purifies them from 92% to 99%. Both companies have adopted chemical purification methods.

China entered this field through technology acquisition and its own R&D, through companies such as GCL (保利协鑫) and LDK (赛维). GCL achieved electronic grade polysilicon (a higher standard than solar grade polysilicon) in 2010. In 2011 its annual polysilicon capacity was among the world's highest.

In the midstream, China and Taiwan were the main players. Of the top ten solar cell producers in 2013, six were based in China and three in Taiwan. First Solar in the USA was the only thin film supplier as well as the only non-Chinese/Taiwanese cell maker in the ranking list. The top ten PV cell suppliers accounted for 40% of global PV cell production in 2013, and 76% of 2013 global PV cell production came from Chinese and Taiwanese crystalline silicon cell suppliers. China gained absolute advantages in PV module production; of the top ten companies in terms of PV modules, seven are from China and Sharp Solar (Japan), Kyocera (Japan) and First Solar (USA) were the only three non-Chinese makers in the ranking in 2013. Yingli took the first position in both PV cell and PV module production in 2013.

The downstream PV deployment process was dominated by Germany, Italy, the USA and Japan due to the early introduction of this technology to their markets. In 2013 Asian countries became the fastest growth area in terms of PV installation, especially China which achieved the largest installation figure of 11.3 GW, followed by Japan with 6.9 GW.

9.4 PV industry in China

In the 2000s the worldwide PV industry enjoyed an explosive growth. In 1999 there was less than 700 MW PV capacity globally; in 2013 more than 37 GW of PV was installed globally, leading to a cumulated PV installed capacity of 139.6 GW (see Figure 9.2).

China entered the PV industry in 2001 when the global market was just emerging. After 2007, China surpassed Japan and Germany, becoming the largest solar module producer in the world, although only a small amount was for domestic consumption. In 2011, China produced more than 20 GW of solar modules accounting for 60% of global production, about 10% of which were installed in China. The price of solar cells decreased dramatically from RMB 45/WP in 2000 to RMB 4.2/WP in 2013 (see Figure 9.3 for the figures between 2007 and 2013).

In recent years, thanks to government incentive plans, China has become the largest PV market. China's installed capacity has shown

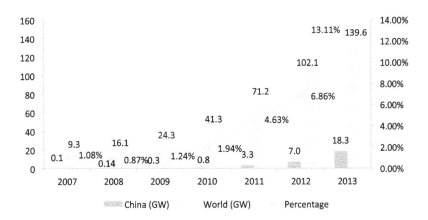

FIGURE 9.2   China's cumulative installed PV capacity as a percentage of the world's total, 2007–13

Source: Cumulative Installed Solar Photovoltaic Capacity in Leading Countries and the World, 2000–2013. Retrieved from http://www.earth-policy.org/datacenter/xls/book_tgt_solar_2.xlsx.

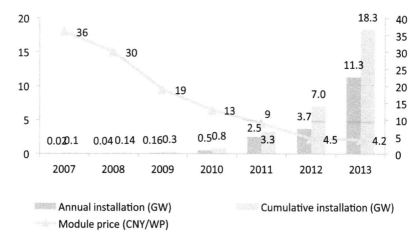

FIGURE 9.3   China's annual and cumulative PV installation with annual module price

Sources: Cumulative Installed Solar Photovoltaic Capacity in Leading Countries and the World, 2000–2013, retrieved from http://www.earth-policy.org/datacenter/xls/book_tgt_solar_2.xlsx; International Energy Agency, *2013 IEA PVPS Annual Report*, retrieved from http://www.iea-pvps.org/index.php?id=6&eID=dam_frontend_push&docID=2040.

a dramatic increase in recent years, from over 0.8 GW in 2010 to 3 GW in 2011, achieving the world's largest installed figure with 11.3 GW in 2013, which accounted for 30% of world's newly installed capacity in that year (see Figures 9.2 and 9.3). Along with the rapid development of China's solar PV industry, there have emerged a number of PV industrial giants including Yingli, Trina Solar and GCL.

The PV industry in China has experienced periodical industrial adjustments and is deeply influenced by both domestic and foreign government policies. Until 2002, China's PV industry remained in the R&D and trial production stage. PV products had not been used for civil applications. In 2002 the then SDPC (State Development Planning Commission, currently the National Development and Reform Commission, NDRC) enacted a Power Supply Plan for Rural Areas without Electricity in the Western Provinces and Regions, which provided a solution for remote areas where there is a lack of power supply.

In 2004, several countries including Germany took the lead, implementing high feed-in tariff (FIT) and PV subsidy policies that stimulated the international PV market. Chinese firms seized the opportunity, expanded their capacity and reduced their production costs through economics of scale. In 2006, the Chinese government launched a series of national policies and regulations such as the Renewable Energy Law, which created a favourable policy environment for the rapid development of China's solar PV industry.

Between 2004 and 2008, China's PV industry developed quickly. For example, the capacity of PV cells expanded at a rate of over 100%; however, almost all the PV modules were exported. The European market played a substantial role in its growth in the 2000s, accounting for around 80% of China's PV exports.

In early 2009, China's exports, including PV products, dropped sharply in response to the economic recession following the 2008 financial crisis. The Ministry of Finance, Ministry of Science and Technology (MOST), National Energy Administration (NEA) and other departments initiated "Large-scale PV Power Station Concession Bidding" and the Golden-Sun Pilot Project to stimulate domestic PV demand. The former installed an approximately 4.3 GW large-scale solar power station between 2009 and 2012. The latter supported over 700 different PV power generation projects focused on a user-side distributed PV system and independent PV system for regions without a power supply. Golden-Sun's gross planned installed capacity in mainland China was over 5.8 GW, which played an important role in initiating a domestic PV market, promoting PV technology and eliminating grid-connected policy obstacles.

Solar irradiation zone	PV power plant	Distributed PV benefits	
	FITs scheme (RMB/kWh)	Subsidy for self-consumed PV electricity (RMB/kWh)	Subsidy for surplus PV electricity feedback to grid (RMB/kWh)
Type-I areas	0.90	Retail price of grid electricity +0.42	Wholesale tariff of coal-fired power +0.42
Type-II areas	0.95		
Type-III	1.00		

TABLE 9.2   Feed-in tariffs for PV power plants and subsidy for distributed PV in China

Source: International Energy Agency (2013). *National Survey Report of PV Power Applications in China 2013.*

Note: The applicable feed-in tariff in Tibet will be decided separately in another policy.

Type-I areas: Ningxia; Haixi of Qinghai Province; Jiayuguan, Wuwei, Zhangye, Jiuquan, Dunhuang, Jinchang of Gansu Province; Hami, Tacheng, Aertai, Kelamayi of Xinjiang Province; Inner Mongolia.

Type-II areas: Beijing; Tianjin; Heilongjiang; Jilin; Liaoning; Sichuan; Yunnan; Chifeng, Tongliao, Xinganmeng, Hulunbeier in Inner Mongolia; Chengde, Zhangjaikou, Tangshan, Qinhuangdao of Hebei Province; Datong, Suzhou, Yizhou of Shangxi Province; Yulin, Yanan of Shannxi Province; places other than the Type-I areas in Qinghai, Gansu and Xinjiang.

Type-III: For areas other than the above.

Affected by the financial crisis, Germany reduced its subsidy in 2011. The USA and the European Union initiated an anti-dumping and anti-subsidy trade investigation into China and, coupled with the overcapacity by domestic stimulation and low-price competition, China's whole PV industry suffered between 2011 and 2013. Several PV enterprises went bankrupt or were reorganized worldwide; the previous industry leader, Suntech Power (尚德), went bankrupt in March 2013. However, in late 2013 China's PV industry had recovered steadily, the recovery driven by Japan's strong feed-in tariff (FIT) policy, a settlement between China and the EU, and a series of supporting policies from the State Council.

One particularly important financial policy was the new FIT scheme, announced in 2013. The scheme split the country into three different areas based on levels of sunshine and construction costs, and offered a differentiated FIT rate for each region. In principle, the price is fixed for 20 years. The detailed FITs can be seen in Table 9.2. Meanwhile, the NEA adjusted the accumulative installed PV capacity target from 21 GW to 35 GW by 2015 for the 12th Five-Year Plan (2011–15).

9.5 Yingli's vertical integration strategy

Yingli was established in Baoding, Hebei province in China in 1998 by Mr Liansheng Miao. In its second year, MOST was trying to engage in solar power generation technology and planned to establish a 3 MW demonstration project. Yingli applied it and finished the project in 2003. Yingli accumulated related module production experience.

In 2004, Yingli decided to establish its ingot, wafer and cell production plants. In the same year, Yingli's cell products received international certifications such as UL, TUV and IEC.[1] With the help of the certifications Yingli began its journey to become a global company and delivered its first international order to Germany. In total Yingli gained 6MW ingot, wafer and cell production capacity, and 50 MW module capacity in 2004. In 2006, Yingli further expanded its production capacity with 95 MW ingot and wafer production capacity, 60 MW cell production capacity and a 100 MW module capacity. In 2012, the production capacity for each

---

[1] UL stands for Underwriter Laboratories Inc., IEC stands for International Electro Technical Commission and TUV stands for Technischer Überwachüngs-Verein ("Technical Inspection Association" in English). The three certifications are recognized in different regions: UL is recognized in the USA, TUV is recognized by Germany and other European countries and IEC is recognized at a global level.

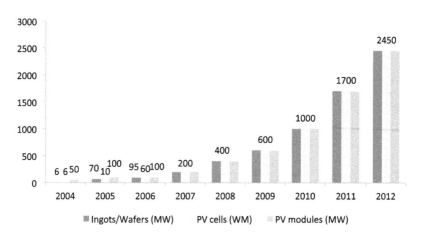

FIGURE 9.4   Yingli production capacity roadmap

Source: http://www.yinglisolar.com/en/about/.

increased to 2.45 GW (see Figure 9.4 for an overview of Yingli's capacity roadmap).

In 2013, Yingli and GCL China signed a strategic cooperation contract (英利与保利协鑫战略合作框架协议) in which the two giants agreed to capitalize each other's advantages. GCL, headquartered in both Shanghai and Hong Kong, is the largest polysilicon supplier in China. It is also involved in wafer production, solar power plants construction and investment.

Yingli set up an internal purchasing company which helps source and purchase the critical materials such as polysilicon, and also direct material such as glass and EVA.[2] Only materials suitable for local sourcing were purchased by local plants. The purchasing company makes purchasing plans, decides the overall purchasing

2   EVA stands for "ethylene vinyl acetate", and is the copolymer of ethylene and vinyl acetate, used in the photovoltaics industry as an encapsulation material for crystalline silicon solar cells in the manufacture of photovoltaic modules.

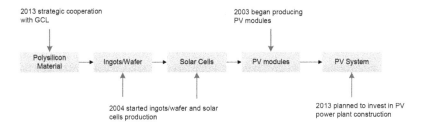

FIGURE 9.5   Yingli vertical integration PV value chain

quantity and allocates to each plant. In 2012, Chinese solar cells were levied with anti-dumping and anti-subsidy duties by the USA; however, this case was open to a third-country loophole as the petition covered only the solar cells made on the Chinese mainland. The purchasing company therefore facilitated the purchase of solar cells from Taiwan, benefiting from its economic status, and avoiding potential penalty.

Yingli's four plants are all vertically integrated and cover ingot casting and wafering, solar cell production and module assembly, which further reduces its transportation costs and enhances the coordination between the value chain processes. Through vertical integration from polysilicon production to ingot, wafer, cell and module production, Yingli not only avoids the volatile price in the market by internalizing the production knowledge of the whole chain, but also greatly reduces polysilicon cost and enhances its profit margins. In addition, integrated production reduces the environmental costs of transportation, breakage and packaging, while providing strict quality control measures at all stages of its manufacturing processes eliminates redundancies, ensures continuous process improvement and cost optimization and reduces carbon emissions.

In 2013, Yingli announced its investment in downstream PV deployment, instead of subcontracting the engineering projects.

Beyond PV module sales, Yingli has been actively involved in the development of downstream PV power plants and EPC (engineering, procurement and construction) projects (Refer to Figure 9.5 for Yingli's vertical value chain strategy). Yingli also created a variety of cooperation models with its partners for its downstream business, such as setting up joint ventures with giants of traditional industry for the development of PV power plants, and establishing a renewable energy fund with China's leading investment fund to invest in solar projects, to offset the large capital demand of PV projects.

9.6 Yingli's R&D activities

Yingli has dedicated itself to a strong R&D programme. As mentioned above, improving solar module efficiencies is an important goal for the PV industry. This means holding down the unit cost, and is also a way to reduce energy consumption and carbon emission. In 2009, Yingli cooperated with the Energy Research Centre of the Netherlands on its PANDA solar cell, and also jointly developed a production line for the PANDA cells with Amtech in the Netherlands. The PANDA cell achieved a 19.8% efficiency conversion rate on the commercial line, and assembled modules from these cells achieved 17.2% efficiency. Yingli worked with Yingkou Yongli, an aluminium frame supplier, to make frames thinner and save material cost.

   In 2010 Yingli set up its national PV key laboratory, accredited and supported by the Chinese government. In 2011 Yingli established the PV industry's largest R&D and after-sales service centre in Spain, providing comprehensive product evaluation, testing and service and helping to guarantee the optimal quality of the PV modules in the European market. In the same year Yingli also established an R&D centre in San Francisco to provide comprehensive product testing, including PV module characterization, reliability and outdoor performance testing, BOS evaluations, system modelling and so on. Yingli believes that the benefits of the two overseas R&D centres are twofold: the research centres are geographically closer to its main consumer countries, and the advanced technologies developed there allow the company to enjoy knowledge spillover effects.

As of April 2014, Yingli has a total of 698 issued patents in China, along with 342 patent applications. From 2010 to 2013, Yingli increased R&D spending by more than 100%.

Yingli is also willing to share innovation achievements with its peers. Every year the company organizes a science and technology fair, to demonstrate big innovation projects or projects with big savings or significant results. Suppliers, customers and industrial peers are all invited. These fairs have two aims: to advertise Yingli's progress, and to provide an opportunity for group learning.

9.7 Yingli sustainable value chain initiatives

> Yingli is committed to transforming cutting-edge technologies into high-performance products and to providing affordable renewable energy for people. While pursuing this target, we have been constantly reducing energy consumption and GHG emissions in our productions and operations in order to provide GREENER and CLEANER solar electricity for everyone.
>
> Mr Liansheng Miao, Chairman and CEO of Yingli

By June 2014, Yingli had provided more than 10 GW of high-quality solar (PV) panels to customers worldwide. Each year, the panels will offset approximately 6.8 million tons of carbon emissions when compared with conventional coal generation, which is equivalent to planting more than 340 million trees. Yingli published its first global sustainability report in May 2013, outlining the company's sustainability practices and targets. Jean Tian, Director of Investor Relations at Yingli, said:

> Overall our company is a leader in the industry in many aspects, not only in market share and brand awareness, but also we continuously enhance our industry influence through our product quality, we are the industrial leader in both technology innovation and corporate social responsibility.

In a green energy industry, Yingli feels it is not enough to just power the world with clean solar energy; it has an added obligation to ensure it maintains high environmental standards in its own operations and its value chain. Yingli has focused on sustainability to differentiate itself from competitors.

In 2009, Yingli became the first Chinese PV company to join the European PV CYCLE Association. Yingli is committed to achieving 100% recycling of retired modules in order to minimize the environmental impact of end-of-life products. For small quantities of modules (fewer than 40), a removal technician will take the end-of-life PV modules to a collection point where they are properly disposed of. After a certain amount of modules are accumulated, they are collected and taken to a recycling plant. For large quantities of modules (more than 40), an on-site collection service is available to take end-of-life PV modules directly to a recycling plant.

In 2012, Yingli became the world's first PV company to obtain Product Carbon Footprint Verification from the TUV Rheinland Group, a highly respected worldwide provider of technical services in the solar industry. This is a method of assessing whole life-cycle GHG emissions. In August 2014 Yingli once again gained Product Carbon Footprint Verification from TUV. The verification helped

Yingli win bids for large-scale government projects in Europe (for example, in France).

9.8 WWF Climate Savers programme

On 29 January 2013, Yingli became the first Chinese company and the first PV manufacturer to join WWF's Climate Savers programme.

Yingli's major Climate Savers commitments include, by the end of 2015:

- To reduce GHG emissions intensity per megawatt (MW) of solar (PV) panel production by 13% from 2010 levels (Scope 1 and 2: direct emissions and indirect emissions from the consumption of electricity and heat)

- To reduce GHG emissions from purchased goods and services per MW of solar (PV) panel production by 7% from 2010 levels (Scope 3 emissions)

- To reduce GHG emissions intensity from upstream transportation by 10% from 2010 levels (Scope 3 emissions)

- To increase its share of renewable energy consumption to at least 4% (and strive to reach 8%) (Scope 4 renewable energy consumption)

In addition, Yingli initiated the launch of a Global Green Solar PV Manufacturing Standard (Scope 5 Global Green Solar PV Manufacturing Standard) with the support of WWF, which aims to promote energy consumption reduction in the PV industry, increase utilization percentage of renewable energy and reduce GHG emissions. The objective is that by the end of 2015 the standard will be fully established, and 50% of global solar manufacturers will have adopted this standard by 2020. Yingli has been closely involved in the development of China's PV industry standards, and that experience should help Yingli to reach this target. "China has global manufacturing leaders, is beginning to have global innovation leaders, and now is beginning to have global leaders in the fight against climate change as well," said Peter Beaudoin, CEO of WWF China.

In May 2014, Yingli began internal inspections to ensure it met its aggressive emission reduction targets. Using 2010 GHG emissions as a baseline, the inspection results demonstrated that Yingli:

- Decreased its GHG emissions intensity per MW of PV module production by approximately 22% in 2013, as compared with its initial target to reduce emissions intensity by 13% by the end of 2015 (Scopes 1 and 2)

- Decreased GHG emissions from purchased goods and services per MW of PV modules production by approximately 12%, as compared with its initial target to reduce emissions by 7% (Scope 3)

- Decreased its GHG emissions from upstream transportation by approximately 17%, as compared with its initial target to reduce emissions by 10% (Scope 3)

To accomplish Scopes 1 and 2, Yingli made significant investments in information technology systems, such as a GHG management platform to monitor and manage energy consumption at each production site. Actions are required to meet the consumption target, which will also help to reduce carbon emissions. Yingli is also trying to increase employee awareness of the importance of energy efficiency and establish a systematic approach for driving improvements across all facilities. An example is "grass-roots innovation", driven by employees with the aim of reducing working time, saving raw materials and reducing energy consumption. Employees are rewarded for their contributions to these goals.

Yingli applied a three-step strategy to improve energy efficiency:

1. Reduction, such as reducing the operation time of the ingot furnace and optimizing water pump operation

2. Improving efficiency, such as purchasing high-efficiency equipment and improving pure water transformation rate

3. Reuse, such as reusing the heat collected from air compressors during their operation

Yingli also realized that its social and environmental impact extends beyond its own operations. A significant portion of the energy and emissions footprint associated with Yingli comes from upstream and downstream activities (Scope 3). Therefore, Yingli will launch a "Green Supplier Action" programme, requiring all of its Tier 1 suppliers to adopt ambitious energy efficiency and GHG reduction commitments. Meanwhile, levels of energy consumption and emissions will become an important criterion for Yingli when selecting qualified suppliers. One initiative to reduce emissions through its value chain will see Yingli work together with its suppliers to promote Forest Stewardship Council (FSC) certification of packaging materials.

In terms of Scope 4, Yingli has actively invested in PV power projects and installed solar power systems to power its PV module manufacturing facilities, including the plants in Baoding Headquarters, Tianjin, Hengshui and Haikou, as well as other buildings, in order to increase the share of renewable electricity in its total power consumption. Yingli aimed for renewable energy to account for at least 4% of the total energy consumption in the production of its PV modules by the end of 2015. Yingli currently owns and operates more than 20 MW of solar projects to power its own solar panel manufacturing facilities.

PV projects in which Yingli had invested by the end of 2013 are estimated to generate approximately 167.85 GWh of clean electricity annually, and the solar energy systems installed on its facilities could generate 39.3 GWh of electricity annually, equivalent to 4.05% of its total power consumption in 2013, achieving the 2015 target. The figure of 4% looks small, but at present solar energy only comprises around 1% of China's energy consumption portfolio and in that context Yingli's achievement is remarkable.

"We know that cutting carbon emissions and spurring economic growth can go hand in hand. Through conducting a series of activities to accomplish our Climate Savers commitments, we will also be able to effectively reduce our energy consumption and further enhance our cost advantages," said Mr Jingfeng Xiong, Vice President and Chief Climate Officer of Yingli, who is responsible for Yingli's energy-saving strategy, reducing GHG emissions, and innovation and investment for related products. "We nominated our Chief Climate Officer, and put the Climate Savers project under our Integrated Resource Reuse Committee: from these two top organizational structures one can see our focus on carbon reduction," added Jean Tian.

9.9 The final word

In June 2014 an article, "World Cup Sponsorship: Yingli Who?" published by *The Economist* questioned why Yingli sponsored the World Cup. Yingli is much smaller than other sponsors in terms of both market value and revenues, and it has also posted nearly three

Item	2010	2011	2012	2013
Cell capacity (MW)	1,000	1,700	2,450	3,200
Module shipment (MW)	1,061.6	1,603.8	2,297.1	3,234.3
Revenue (in millions)	US$1,896.9	US$2,332.1	US$1,828.5	US$2,216.4
Net income (in millions)	US$210.4	−US$509.8	−US$491.9	−US$321.2

TABLE 9.3   Yingli's financial status

Source: http://www.nasdaq.com/symbol/yge/financials.

straight years of losses. Yingli's annual financial data can be found in Table 9.3. Yingli responded:

> As one of the world's leading solar panel manufacturers, Yingli has committed to converting boundless solar energy into green energy for all. The World Cup is the world's most prominent sports event and a perfect platform for us to help everyone to learn more about how using solar energy can be integral to achieving global sustainability. The evolution of the world's PV markets, distributed generation segment and new merging markets, including Africa and South America, are playing an increasingly important role. Through the World Cup, we have made Yingli Solar known in millions of homes, which resulted in the increase of our brand awareness, customer base and sales.
>
> Qing Miao, VP Corporate Communications, Yingli

Yingli's PV module shipment in 2013 doubled compared with 2011, but its annual revenue in 2013 was slightly smaller than in 2011, reflecting the continuous price reduction of PV modules and the fierce competition among PV manufacturers. Although Yingli's reported losses reduced, the company still needs to improve the health of its finances. After surviving several rounds of industrial adjustments, a question remains: how far will Yingli go with its vertical value chain integration and sustainable strategy?

9.10 Case summary

As a leading solar energy company, Yingli has, along with similar companies, had to overcome the challenge posed by energy suppliers from traditional sources such as coal and oil. As well as innovating to make its products more affordable, Yingli has created a "Green Supplier Action Programme" to encourage sustainability throughout its value chain. Key features include:

- Investing in photovoltaic power projects and using solar power to power its own headquarters, manufacturing plants and other facilities

- Setting targets for use of renewable energy in the production of solar panels

- Requiring all Tier 1 suppliers to adopt ambitious energy efficiency and greenhouse gas reduction commitments

- Working together with suppliers to promote Forest Stewardship Council certified packaging materials

Conclusion
The role of supply chain leadership in achieving SSCM leadership: an academic perspective

Based on the nine Climate Savers case studies, it seems that in practice, major Western-based multinational corporations (MNCs) respond proactively to the constraints of scarce resources and environmental degradation, usually claim to integrate sustainability as part of their strategy and tend to assume a leadership role in their supply chains in order to implement various practices aiming at improved sustainability along with quality, price and reliability.

The idea that a supply chain competes with other supply chains is not new and there is an increasing body of literature on SSCM. These emerging "sustainable" practices involve dissemination or learning or knowledge transfer of new ideas throughout a supply chain, thereby influencing wider networks. For example, Tetra Pak disseminates its sustainability practice to both upstream (buying FSC-certified wood products) and downstream supply chains (educating Mengniu and Yili on sustainability). The fundamental questions are:

- What are the SSCM strategies available to MNCs?
- What is the role of MNCs in achieving sustainable supply chains in China?

SSCM strategies

Van Tulder *et al.* (2009) propose that implementing codes of conduct was a "trendy" SSCM strategy five or six years ago, but nowadays it is generally a minimum requirement and has become an industry standard approach (Gimenez and Sierra, 2013). After van Tulder, Closs *et al.* (2011) classify firms adopting SSCM into reactor, contributor and innovator and Harms *et al.* (2013) classify SSCM strategy into risk-oriented or opportunity-oriented; however, both classifications mainly focus on a focal company perspective.

Gosling *et al.* (2015) propose a new classification of reactive, contributive and proactive SSCM strategies from both buyer and supplier perspectives, building on previous works (Closs *et al.*, 2011; van Tulder *et al.*, 2009). Focal companies implementing a reactive strategy focus on efficiency and primary stakeholders mainly by setting up a low level of the code of conduct with which suppliers are required to comply, but make few efforts beyond compliance. All the case study companies in this book have been implementing this strategy for noncritical items which they outsource.

Going one step ahead, focal firms adopting a contributive SSCM strategy recognize SSCM as strategically important and take a more proactive initiative by benchmarking within or across industry to identify potential approaches and collaborate with suppliers.

However, these initiatives are normally not their own creation. Active SSCM strategy requires focal companies to initiate SSCM projects with their existing knowledge and then actively involve, train and develop selected suppliers or the whole supply chain. Many of the case study companies have also adopted this strategy for some categories of the purchased items. For example, Nestlé does this based on their existing knowledge of coffee-growing techniques to develop coffee growers and companies.

Going even further, focal firms adopting a proactive SSCM strategy consider SSCM a strategic priority and a long-term investment, eagerly seeking best practices through innovation. Proactive SSCM strategy emphasizes the deep and close collaboration between focal companies and specific suppliers with the aim of jointly innovating sustainable products, processes or business modes. Tetra Pak adopts this strategy in creating a recycling supply chain in China. On the one hand, they engaged with local government stakeholders and China Packaging Association to create a waste carton collection system, which is one of the two keys to the success of recycling. On the other hand, Tetra Pak introduced the idea of separation of aluminium and paper in the packaging and financed and collaborated with SME start-ups to co-develop the technology. Tetra Pak also helped develop a market for the recycled products of these SMEs, which is considered another key to the success of recycling.

It should be noted that the clear distinction we have drawn between the three types of SSCM strategy is for purposes of theory development. In reality, MNCs employ a range of different approaches that transcend the three alternatives suggested. For instance, Walmart uses standard reactive SSCM strategies to enforce their basic code of conduct.

Seuring and Muller (2008) define SSCM as "The management of material, information and capital flows as well as cooperation among companies along the supply chain while taking goals from all three dimensions of sustainable development, i.e. economic, environmental, and social, into account which are derived from customers and stakeholder requirements." This definition focuses on achieving three goals – economic, environment and social – derived from stakeholders' requirements. In our view, all three types of SSCM strategy can be considered as achieving the three SSCM goals but at different degrees. The reactive strategy aims to comply with a basic code of conduct meeting minimum requirements from all the stakeholders; contributive strategy tends to be more proactive and attempts to improve SSCM performance within the existing framework to benefit stakeholders; finally, proactive strategy is the most proactive of the three and intends to surprise and even educate stakeholders and achieve goals beyond their expectations.

Role of MNCs in achieving SSCM

Based on the nine MNC case studies, we can clearly observe that these multinationals play a leading role in disseminating or implementing SSCM practice in their supply chains in China. Defee *et al.* (2009a) suggest that a supply chain is a complex organizational network which requires leadership from a supply chain leader organization to drive changes for the whole chain and conclude that transformational supply chain leadership can enhance the development of closed-loop supply chain orientation. In this section, we attempt to discuss the supply chain leadership concept and its consequences and then link them to the case studies.

In the literature, power and collaboration are two opposing streams of research in buyer–supplier relationships in which collaboration has prevailed in recent years. However, to manage a supplier relationship, power is an unavoidable topic. Existing literatures

(Cooper *et al.*, 1997; Cox, 2001; Cox *et al.*, 2004; Stevens, 1989) tend not to distinguish power and leadership and sometimes use power as a proxy for leadership. For example, Hall (2000) claims that power can be applied by channel leaders to influence suppliers towards sustainability. Power has been introduced in market channel literatures to describe how any industry is probably dominated by two or three major competitors (Daugherty, 2011). The exercise of power or lack of power can affect the level of commitment of other channel members; however, forced participation will encourage exit behaviour if given the opportunity (Cooper *et al.*, 1997). Cox (2001) and Cox *et al.* (2004) discuss the different types of power relationship between buyers and suppliers.

However, Ahi and Searcy (2013) stress the voluntary character of SSCM and claim that power may not be able to fully explain proactive SSCM behaviours. Focal companies collaborate with suppliers on SSCM initiatives, in which suppliers may be driven by the leader's sustainable vision, a characteristic of leadership (Ahi and Searcy, 2013). Echoing this, Defee *et al.* (2009a) argue that power should not be viewed as the sole source of supply chain leadership; other aspects of leadership should be taken into consideration. Defee *et al.* (2010, p. 766) further propose a formal definition of supply chain leadership:

> a relational concept involving the supply chain leader and one or more supply chain follower organizations that interact in a dynamic, co-influencing process. The supply chain leader is characterized as the organization that demonstrates higher levels of the four elements of leadership in relation to other member organizations (i.e. the organization capable of greater influence, readily identifiable by its behaviours, creator of the vision, and that establishes a relationship with other supply chain organizations).

In terms of leadership categorization and in the more limited literature on supply chain leadership, the majority of papers focus on transactional and/or transformational leadership styles (Defee *et al.*, 2009a, 2009b, 2010; Hult and Nichols, 1999; Hult *et al.*, 2000a, 2000b). Defee *et al.* (2009b) argue that both transactional and transformational leadership operate via contingent reward and management by exception, while transformational leadership more frequently exhibits inspiration, intellectual stimulation and individualized consideration. Contingent reward indicates that followers will be rewarded on their expected performance, management by exception implies that leaders point out followers' mistakes and take actions when needed (Bass and Avolio, 2000).

Defee *et al.* (2009a) explain inspirational behaviour as an articulation of a collective mission; a vision of desirable futures and the definition of the path to achieve the vision. Intellectual stimulation occurs where leaders call on followers to be more innovative and creative to provide better solutions to problems. Individualized consideration refers to a leader's ability to recognize each individual follower's unique skills and development needs. Transformational leaders focus on developing long-term relationships and do not seek to control followers' behaviour through the use of contingent rewards, but manage in a more holistic way (Avolio *et al.*, 1988; Bass, 1985).

Harland *et al.* (2007) argue that the fact that downstream larger businesses don't assume supply chain leadership poses a barrier for SMEs adopting e-Business (information technology-based business). Defee *et al.* (2009a) claim that transformational supply chain leadership moderates the relationship between sustainability drivers and closed-loop supply chain orientation. Transformational leadership is also found to positively influence organizational learning (Hult *et al.*, 2000b). There is also a positive relationship between transformational leadership and organizational performance such as purchasing cycle time (Hult and Nichols, 1999; Hult *et al.*, 2000b), efficiency and effectiveness (Defee *et al.*, 2009b, 2010).

According to these case study companies, it seems that they more or less play a critical role in their supply chains in China. Tetra Pak assumed transformational leadership in a dairy supply chain in pushing the student milk programme and setting up a recycling supply chain for its waste cartons by inspiring Mengniu, Yili and small garbage collectors and recyclers towards social and environmental sustainability. Fairmont educates its customers regarding the local ecosystem. Nestlé inspires farmers and governmental agencies in Pu'er to produce good food (coffee) and live a good life, improving the living standards of local communities significantly. Some companies (SKF, Volvo Group and Sony) adopt a more transactional leadership style by rewarding the good practice and punishing non-compliance in environmental and social sustainability. Vanke also assumes a transactional leadership in the supply chain by punishing those suppliers who don't comply with international quality standards. HP adopts a mixed leadership style of transactional and transformational because it attempts to inspire the first-tier suppliers to achieve energy efficiency (environmental sustainability) on the one hand and punish those who don't abide by social sustainability (e.g. SA8000) on the other. Yingli doesn't have this issue because it is vertically integrated.

Based on the case studies, we draw two conclusions regarding supply chain leadership:

1. The adoption of appropriate leadership style by MNCs is conducive to the learning of sustainable practice and improving the overall SSCM performance in the supply chain

2. The supply chain leadership style of MNCs tends to change from more transactional at the beginning, to more

transformational when a culture of sustainability is built
in the supply chain

What of the way forward? The pressures on all companies operating in China, but especially foreign-domiciled MNCs, to commit
to sustainable practices will only increase as time passes. The
Chinese central and regional governments have made clear their
commitment to both environmental and social sustainability, and
that commitment is likely to grow; we can, for example, expect still
more stringent restrictions and regulations in the next Five-Year
Plan. Long-term business success in China and commitment to
bettering the environment are likely to go hand in hand. Indeed, in
this respect, China might well turn out to be a world leader, creating
a business climate where profit and responsibility are seen, not as
polar opposites, but as two sides of the same coin.

As the case studies in this book have shown, one area where
companies can demonstrate that commitment is in the design and
management of sustainable supply chains. Not only that, but – as
the case studies in this book also show – by developing sustainable
supply chains companies can also reap significant business benefits
in three key areas:

1. Cost savings

2. An improved image among consumers and customers,
   resulting in greater brand equity

3. Greater levels of trust and commitment on the part of
   partners, who will see the first two benefits replicated in
   their own businesses as they too become more sustainable

The message is clear: it is not a matter of whether companies should
achieve sustainability in their supply chains in China, but how they
are going to do it.

References

Ahi, P., & Searcy, C. (2013). A comparative literature analysis of definitions for green and sustainable supply chain management. *Journal of Cleaner Production*, 52, 329-341.

Avolio, B.J., Waldman, D.A., & Einstein, W.O. (1988). Transformational leadership in a management game simulation. *Group and Organizational Studies*, 13(1), 59-80.

Bass, B.M. (1985). *Leadership and Performance Beyond Expectations*. New York, NY: The Free Press.

Bass, B.M., & Avolio, B.J. (2000). *MLQ Multifactor Leadership Questionnaire* (2nd ed.). Redwood City, CA: Mind Garden.

Closs, D.J., Speier, C., & Meacham, N. (2011). Sustainability to support end-to-end value chains: the role of supply chain management. *Journal of the Academy of Marketing Science*, 39(1), 101-116.

Cooper, M.C., Lambert, D.M., & Pagh, J.D. (1997). Supply chain management: more than a new name for logistics. *The International Journal of Logistics Management*, 8(1), 1-14.

Cox, A. (2001). Understanding buyer and supplier power: a framework for procurement and supply competence. *The Journal of Supply Chain Management*, 37(2), 8-15.

Cox, A., Watson, G., Lonsdale, C., & Sanderson, J. (2004). Managing appropriately in power regimes: relationship and performance management in 12 supply chain cases. *Supply Chain Management: An International Journal*, 9(5), 357-371.

Daugherty, P.J. (2011). Review of logistics and supply chain relationship literature and suggested research agenda. *International Journal of Physical Distribution & Logistics Management*, 41(1), 16-31.

Defee, C.C., Esper, T., & Mollenkopf, D. (2009a). Leveraging closed-loop orientation and leadership for environmental sustainability. *Supply Chain Management: An International Journal*, 14(2), 87-98.

Defee, C.C., Stank, T.P., Esper, T.L., & Mentzer, J.T. (2009b). The role of followers in supply chains. *Journal of Business Logistics*, 30(2), 65-84.

Defee, C.C., Stank, T.P., & Esper, T.L. (2010). Performance implications of transformational supply chain leadership and followership. *International Journal of Physical Distribution & Logistics Management*, 40(10), 763-791.

Gimenez, C., & Sierra, V. (2013). Sustainable supply chains: governance mechanisms to greening suppliers. *Journal of Business Ethics*, 116(1), 189-203.

Gosling, J., Jia, F., Gong, Y., & Brown, S. (2015). The role of supply chain leadership in the learning of sustainable practice: toward an integrated framework. *Journal of Cleaner Production* (in press).

Hall, J. (2000). Environmental supply chain dynamics. *Journal of Cleaner Production*, 8(6), 455-471.

Harland, C.M., Caldwell, N.D., Powell, P., & Zheng, J. (2007). Barriers to supply chain information integration: SMEs adrift of eLands. *Journal of Operations Management*, 25(6), 1234-1254.

Harms, D., Hansen, E.G., & Schaltegger, S. (2013). Strategies in sustainable supply chain management: an empirical investigation of large German companies. *Corporate Social Responsibility and Environmental Management*, 20(4), 205-218.

Hult, G.T.M., & Nichols Jr, E.L. (1999). A study of team orientation in global purchasing. *Journal of Business and Industrial Marketing*, 14(3), 194-210.

Hult, G.T.M., Ferrell, O.C., Hurley, R.F., & Giunipero, L.C. (2000a). Leadership and relationship commitment: a focus on the supplier–buyer–user linkage. *Industrial Marketing Management*, 29(2), 111-119.

Hult, G.T.M., Hurley, R.F., Giunipero, L.C., & Nichols Jr, E.L. (2000b). Organizational learning in global purchasing: a model and test of internal user and corporate buyers. *Decision Sciences*, 31(2), 293-325.

Seuring, S., & Muller, M. (2008). From a literature review to a conceptual framework for sustainable supply chain management. *Journal of Cleaner Production*, 16(15), 1699-1710.

Stevens, G.C. (1989). Integrating the supply chain. *International Journal of Physical Distribution & Logistics Management*, 19(8), 3-8.

van Tulder, R., van Wijk, J., & Kolk, A. (2009). From chain liability to chain responsibility. *Journal of Business Ethics*, 85(2), 399-412.

About the authors

Dr Jeff (Fu) Jia is a Senior Lecturer in Supply Network Management at the University of Exeter, UK. He is a co-founder and director of the Business, Nature and Value research group affiliated to Exeter, which aims to focus on the relationships between business, nature and value creation. Dr Jia's research interests include supply relationship management in a  cross-cultural context, global sourcing, supply chain learning and innovation and sustainable SCM in agricultural and industrial contexts.

Jonathan Gosling is Professor Emeritus at the Centre for Leadership Studies, University of Exeter, UK, and co-founder of the Business, Nature and Value research group, which currently holds grants to study co-ops in international food supply chains and continuing work on green-economy innovations. Recent

research projects include the management of malaria elimination programmes for the Gates Foundation; multi-sector partnerships in flood defence schemes; and the role of corporations in setting the UN Sustainable Development Goals. He is active in the "greening" of management education worldwide and is co-founder of the One Planet MBA and Coachingourselves.com. He is visiting professor at Renmin University, Beijing, and previously worked as a community mediator.

Morgen Witzel is an internationally known writer and lecturer on business and management. He is the author of 23 books, which have been translated into 12 languages. Two of his books, *Doing Business in China* (shortly to appear in its fourth edition) and *Tata: The Evolution of a Corporate Brand*, have been international bestsellers. His articles have appeared in the *Financial Times*, *Financial World*, *The Smart Manager*, *EFMD Global Quarterly* and many others. For the past 12 years he has taught at the University of Exeter Business School, UK, and has been part of the teaching faculty group for the One Planet MBA programme. He is a Fellow of the University's Centre for Leadership Studies and a Fellow of the Royal Society of Arts, Manufactures and Commerce.

For Product Safety Concerns and Information please contact our EU
representative GPSR@taylorandfrancis.com
Taylor & Francis Verlag GmbH, Kaufingerstraße 24, 80331 München, Germany

www.ingramcontent.com/pod-product-compliance
Ingram Content Group UK Ltd.
Pitfield, Milton Keynes, MK11 3LW, UK
UKHW021032180425
457613UK00021B/1136